By Dawn's Early Light

Waterfowl hunting, retrievers, and other
aspects of morning madness

E. Donnall Thomas Jr.

DUCKS UNLIMITED, INC.
Memphis, Tennessee

Book Design: Monte Clair Finch

Published by Ducks Unlimited, Inc.
L. J. Mayeux, President
Julius Wall, Chairman of the Board
D. A. (Don) Young, Executive Vice President

ISBN: 1-57223-407-5

Published April 2001

Ducks Unlimited, Inc.
The mission of Ducks Unlimited is to fulfill the annual life cycle needs
of North American waterfowl by protecting, enhancing, restoring, and
managing important wetlands and associated uplands. Since its found-
ing in 1937, DU has raised more than $1.3 billion, which has con-
tributed to the conservation of over 9.4 million acres of prime wildlife
habitat in all fifty states, each of the Canadian provinces, and in key
areas of Mexico. In the U.S. alone, DU has helped to conserve over 2
million acres of waterfowl habitat. Some 900 species of wildlife live
and flourish on DU projects, including many threatened and endan-
gered species.

Library of Congress Cataloging-in-Publication Data
Thomas, E. Donnall
    By dawn's early light : waterfowl hunting, retrievers, and other
    aspects of morning madness / E. Donnall Thomas, Jr.
        p. cm.
        ISBN 1-57223-407-5 (alk. paper)
        1. Waterfowl shooting--Anecdotes. I. Title.
    SK331 .T56 2001
    799.2'44--dc21

                                                    2001017500

For Nicole and Scott

Call to Action

The success of Ducks Unlimited hinges upon each member's personal involvement in the conservation of North America's wetlands and waterfowl. You can help Ducks Unlimited meet its conservation goals by volunteering your time, energy, and resources; by participating in our conservation programs; and by encouraging others to do the same. To learn more about how you can make a difference for the ducks, call 1-800-45-DUCKS.

TABLE OF CONTENTS

Other Books by the Author

Longbows in the Far North
Whitefish Can't Jump
Longbow Country
Dream Fish and Road Trips
Fool Hen Blues
To All Things a Season
The Double Helix
The Life of a Lab
Labs Afield

FOREWORD

If you spend any time at all reading magazines—any type of magazines—you'll see a little design element called a pull quote. This is a particularly salient sentence or phrase that the editor feels captures the essence of the story, something that will spur the reader to want to read the piece, or maybe just an enchanting bit of prose that will spice up the design of the page. It's normally run big and often in color, in a box, with quote marks around it.

When I am editing one of Don Thomas's stories for either *The Retriever Journal* or *The Pointing Dog Journal* magazines, to which he regularly contributes, I'll sometimes spend an hour with my little yellow highlighter poised over the manuscript trying to pick out a pull quote. Why? Because I could highlight the whole damn story.

Don Thomas is one of the continent's best outdoor writers—no, make that essayists. He is also one of the most prolific and widely published. He writes on bowhunting and flyfishing and upland hunting. And waterfowling, the subject of this book. Don enjoys the rugged life, and duck and goose hunting and riding herd on his three generations of

Labs certainly qualifies. You may have one or more of his Labrador retriever coffee-table books, also published by DU.

A physician by education and a writer by choice, Don samples the sporting smorgasbord like almost no one I know; he's an accomplished shotgunner, fly fisherman, and bowhunter—one of the country's best and most well known, in fact. He regularly travels from his home in Montana to Africa, Alaska (where he once lived), and a lot of points in between for sport. His long-suffering wife, Lori, has thrown up her hands in surrender and has taken her place as his nearly constant outdoor companion, the theory being, I would guess, that if you can't beat 'em, join 'em...provided you can find 'em.

As proof of that last statement, I just got a message from Don that he was home for a while after a trip to Quebec but would be leaving for Mozambique in a couple days. Or maybe it was the other way around. I forget.

As you read this book, it will become clear to you—if you haven't tasted his work before—that Don Thomas is what we have too few of in the outdoor writing business: a sensitive, introspective, highly skilled sportsman who cares for the birds, the dogs, and what someone once called "the gentlemanly comings and goings" of the sporting life.

—*Steve Smith*
Traverse City, Michigan

Acknowledgments

Somewhat different versions of parts of this text have appeared previously in the following publications: chapters 1, 7, and 15: *Ducks Unlimited*; chapter 2: *Retriever Journal*; chapter 5: *Gray's Sporting Journal*; chapter 8: *Shooting Sportsman*; part of chapter 10: *Alaska*.

The author appreciates the opportunity to rework the material for inclusion in this volume.

LAST FLIGHT

An experienced air traveler himself, Sky, my old yellow Lab, sat patiently in the back seat of the Super Cub as we emerged from the confining walls of Lake Clark Pass and started across the tide flats of Cook Inlet toward home. It had already been a long day of flying, but the October sun's oblique rays seemed to have set the world on fire beneath us, and the golden glow that spread across the grass proved too compelling to ignore. Waterfowl dotted the potholes underneath the wings as we descended toward the deck, confirming my decision to let home and all the responsibilities attending it wait until another day.

My first turn over the duck cabin revealed no evidence of any of my hunting partners, a discovery that produced mixed feelings. While I'm often happy to hunt alone, few places enforce the value of companionship quite like the northern bush, and after a long day beyond the Alaska

Range I frankly would have appreciated some human company. But when I set up and landed in the grass beside the little shack, I felt no regrets as the engine died and the silence of the place rose up to greet me. This was the end of the season, and in some ways it felt best to close things down on my own, with no one around other than the dog. Besides, no one can really say they're alone while in the presence of a Labrador retriever.

A marvel of crude construction, the duck cabin consisted of little more than a fifteen-foot-square wooden box on stilts meant to survive the inlet's flood tides and provide a simple means of shelter when we visited. Despite its humble specs, the cabin offered a nearly immeasurable sense of sanctuary. The rule was simple: None of us ever took anything useful away from the duck cabin, and every time one of our party landed there we unloaded the disposable contents of the airplane and left them for the common good. No one kept track of these donations. We were hunters after all, not accountants. A dozen seasons' worth of this positive trade balance had produced a world-class collection of canned food, cheap novels, and odd shotgun shells that always made the place feel as inviting as a second home.

After quickly confirming that the cabin still held everything we needed to survive the night, I walked right back out the door and stared off across the flats, because what I really felt like doing with the remains of the day was shooting some

2

ducks. It only takes one or two Octobers to teach new arrivals in the Great Land just how quickly winter's curtain can fall, and I had learned my own lesson several seasons before. The wealth of open water dotting the flats could yield to ice overnight at that time of year, and I knew that when it did the waterfowl would disappear right along with it. Confident of nothing so much as nature's fickle mood during the brief northern autumn, I dug my shotgun from the back of the Cub and retrieved a box of shells and a sack of decoys from the cabin. Finally, I set off across the flooded grass with the dog at my side, less impressed by the memory of the ducks I had seen from the air than by the magnitude of the emptiness surrounding us.

Sky and I walked for over a mile before we stopped beside a tidal pothole chosen nearly at random. The air lay lifeless over the flats that afternoon and there weren't a lot of ducks moving. The water still tasted faintly of the inlet's last high tide. As I waded out across the mud dropping decoys in my wake, the quavering sound of cranes on the wing spilled down out of the lonely sky, and I paused briefly to determine its source. With my eyes squinted against the light spilling over the peaks to the west, I finally spotted the birds gathered in a towering flock nearly a mile beyond the cabin. They seemed to be reaching for altitude beneath their wings, as if they meant to be airborne for some time, and it occurred to me that perhaps they knew something I didn't.

3

By Dawn's Early Light

With the decoys in place at last, I nestled down in the grass with the dog at my side to enjoy the rest of the afternoon. As the mountains' rugged outline loomed high above the tidal plain behind us, the crisp air magnified the details of their ice-on-rock mosaic as if I were studying them through a telescope. Across the tidal gut in front of the decoys a set of brown bear tracks wandered idly through the mud, too old to ruin my sense of calm but still too fresh to ignore completely. Only in Alaska, I reminded myself. And for a moment it scarcely mattered whether the ducks arrived or not.

But then they did, unannounced, as if by magic, for the weather never stirred to move them. One moment the dog and I felt pleasantly lost in the silence, and then the skies began to fill with wings, as if all the birds in the flyway had suddenly decided they just couldn't stand their own inactivity any longer. The first ducks into the decoy spread were a pair of greenwings that I dropped easily, only to have a dozen mallards try to land on Sky's head during the course of his first retrieve. I shot one drake and ignored the rest. By then it was already obvious that I was about to enjoy an easy limit, and I frankly didn't have much else to do before the sun went down except enjoy the spectacle and the shooting, a process that promised to yield more pleasure extended over time.

During periods of fast action in a duck blind, I find that variety really is the spice of life, a means of appreciating the additional layers of anticipation that ultimately distinguish hunting from target shooting and ducks from clay pigeons. And the slowly darkening skies served up as much variety as anyone could ask for, from wigeon to pintails to goldeneyes. Some I shot and some I let pass by without asking anything other than a brief opportunity to appreciate the sight and sound of them in flight, and I could not have told which I enjoyed more. Even the dog seemed subdued by the furious activity overhead, for he returned to my side after each retrieve and sat patiently, as if he knew the end would come sooner than either of us really wished.

Naïve products of the wilderness, the birds decoyed like fools, and the shooting felt casual and unhurried. I had a limit of ducks resting beside me in half an hour, but I lingered anyway, pretending to be hunting geese or cranes but really doing nothing more than watching and listening to the sound of all those wings overhead. Then the darkness began to rise up out of the tide guts and crawl down across the flats from the mountains and their distant, chilly backlight. Suddenly conscious of the bear tracks, I gathered up the decoys and set off through the grass without bothering to unload the gun. Nightfall in bear country always makes company of any kind feel welcome, and as we walked along through the twilight I found myself welcoming the dog's antics at my side more than I ever imagined possible.

Back at the cabin, I dressed the two greenwings, hung the rest of the birds, saved the teal giblets for the dog, and let the feathers and the guts wash downstream on the outbound tide. There weren't supposed to be any dogs allowed inside the cabin, but I broke the rules, and Sky and I eventually settled down to a meal of seared teal breasts and noodles, in my case, and raw duck livers and dog chow in his. I'm sure I speak for both of us by confiding our immense satisfaction in that simple meal. When I stepped out on the porch for the last time that night I could hear a cacophony of geese moving high overhead. It was hard to avoid the impression that the whole deck was being shuffled somewhere out there in the moonlight. Then I turned down the heat in the oil stove and crawled into the sleeping bag I had pulled out of the Cub's front seat, and settled down to sleep.

I awoke the following morning to the sound of Sky scratching at the door, and a strange visual impression of muted light. The explanation for the dog's restlessness proved simple enough—he had to pee—but the odd quality of the light required a bit of study. A hard frost had coated the cabin's meager windows, and the rising sun lay shrouded in ice fog over the inlet, creating a cool, luminous glow that barely managed to penetrate our little haven. The warmth inside the sleeping bag proved remarkably tempting, but the obvious change in weather had me worried about practical matters, so I crawled out of bed and headed for the porch, despite the temptation to hibernate.

Chapter One • Last Flight

The chill hit me as soon as my feet hit the cabin floor; not even the guttering flame inside the oil stove could deter it. Beyond the door, plates of rime stood in heaps upon the grass while the same potholes that had welcomed us the day before lay seized by ice. Fresh snow covered the mountains and descended toward the flats in windswept swirls, smooth and as evenly textured as whipping cream. The sky overhead remained stubbornly silent. Finally, I realized that the birds were gone—teal, mallards, cranes, geese, all of them—as suddenly and completely as if they had never been there in the first place. They had simply pulled up stakes and left those of us who could not follow to endure what remained behind. But we had enjoyed one final afternoon together, the few birds I shot and the thousands I simply watched fly by. I knew I could depend on the memory of the last afternoon to sustain me during the cold, dark months ahead, just as surely as I could depend on the birds to return again next spring, when I would need to see them again the most. For that I felt an immense gratitude that not even the winter's first honest chill could penetrate.

I spent the morning waiting for the sun to burn a hole through the fog and gauging the cabin's food reserves against the possibility that the dog and I were there to stay for a while. The distant southern sun never really warmed the air, but it finally worried a hole through the ice fog, and when blue sky appeared overhead I closed the place down and fired up the airplane with no small measure of regret. It was over for the year, and even Sky seemed to know it. But as I thought about the noise the departing geese had made the night before, I recognized a central truth: Our last flight of the year would soon be someone else's first.

I could only hope they enjoyed the birds as much as we had.

Chapter Two

DOWN AND DIRTY

The air lay hot and still above the great brackish pan, as if the September sun meant to suck up the last of the swamp water right before our eyes. It was so quiet we could hear muskrats working in the dry reeds behind the blind, and needless to say, the ducks weren't moving. Ray and I had each swatted a couple of bluewings right at first light, but silence had prevailed since then and weather conditions didn't offer any promise of relief. For once, I actually missed the presence of other hunters out in this remote corner of the prairie, for a few more guns scattered about the huge marsh could only have advanced our cause. But there we were on the opening day of duck season, surrounded by prime waterfowl habitat containing thousands of birds, all of which seemed perfectly content to dabble their way through the morning without taking to the air.

After all the anticipation of opening day, it was hard to avoid a general deflation of the spirits as we gathered the decoys and set off through the goo toward the truck. Sky was little more than a puppy then and he found plenty of ways to amuse himself on the long walk back through the reeds, while Ray's Chessie looked hot, bored, and even surlier than usual. But Ray and I knew something the dogs did not, and we weren't ready to write off our opener as a bust until we pursued our final option.

Five miles away toward the distant Missouri, the wetlands' efflux gathered itself into a winding prairie creek, although few trout fisherman would identify it as such. The water there looked as thick and brown as the mud clinging to our waders, and a feather dropped on its surface would more likely move with the wind than the current. Too thick to drink and too thin to plow, the local wisdom went. But we appreciated a special form of beauty in the creek's high banks and sinuous course, for the terrain offered an ideal means of salvaging our opening day: jump-shooting.

Sky didn't look particularly happy about being brought in to heel as we hiked across the grass toward the first bend in the creek, but despite his youth, he already demonstrated the level-headedness that would mark our next decade together, and I didn't have to scold him twice. Thirty yards from the edge of the creek bank, Ray and I began to ooze forward as if we were stalking big game. Suddenly he hesitated, studied the waterline upstream, and began a slow retreat that I quickly joined. After a last-minute review of the landmarks on the opposite bank, we made a wide circle and, in a full state of alert, approached the spot we had marked.

The creek's steep bank proved so well suited to our purpose that, barring some mental breakdown on the part of the dogs, even a careless approach probably would have put us in range. In areas that receive regular hunting pressure, ducks soon learn to avoid such defilades, but this opening day took place in a remote area long ago, and the birds were still unseasoned. As Ray and I slowly approached the bank, the tension level began to rise, as if we were trying to defuse a bomb. Then, suddenly and splendidly, the bomb exploded.

We had seen a few ducks silhouetted against the far bank and had heard the feeding chuckle of contented mallards during the stalk, but neither of us had ever managed a good look at the water below the near bank and we really had no idea what to expect. During our circling approach across the grass, Ray had pantomimed an estimate of ten birds with the fingers of his free hand, a guess that proved low by an order of magnitude. The first bird I saw on the water was a mallard hen tucked in against the opposite bank. As we hove into view, she straightened her neck and stared in disbelief before she sounded off and flushed, triggering a chain reaction that immediately filled the air with a riot of straining wings.

The rise contained a typical early-season mix of Central Flyway puddle ducks, including teal, mallards, and birds of all sizes in between. The first rule in such chaotic circumstances is to identify your target. Since this hunt took place during the old point-system days, and I felt like shooting a lot of ducks, I bore down on a pair of ten-point gadwalls rocketing skyward right in front of me. The second rule is not to miss, not after all that careful maneuvering has put you so close to so many ducks, and I didn't. Not that there was anything difficult about the shooting; the trick was simply to convince myself to isolate one target at a time in the middle of all that confusion.

Such Lord Ripon moments constitute an excellent argument in support of longstanding federal restrictions on magazine capacity while hunting waterfowl. I was shooting my double, and Ray his legally plugged pump, and the five dead birds scattered across the water and the opposite creek bank when the noise settled felt like plenty, especially since I had a young dog to work. Nothing invites a novice retriever's attention quite like a fluffy duck floating belly up in still water, and Ray politely hung onto his Chessie while I directed Sky to the first easy retrieve. Just then, a crazed flock of bluewings barreled around the creek's nearest downstream bend, and Ray, who had maintained the foresight to reload, dropped a pair of them as they flared overhead. At that point, we had too many birds down to worry about etiquette, and we let the dogs collect what remained in the manner they saw fit.

By the time we had all the game safely in hand, my feet had started to swelter inside my hip waders, but I didn't care. It was opening day, and young Sky was hunting like a dream. As I tracked the course of the creek across the shimmering plain to the south, I imagined that every bend held a bounty similar to the one we had just enjoyed. Breakfast could wait; there were ducks to stalk and dogs to work and if our opening day's salvation came courtesy of something other than classical gunning over decoys, no one in our party felt snooty enough to complain.

While decoys, calls, and blinds all lie close to the heart of the waterfowling experience, circumstances don't always allow for their employment. Because of weather, terrain, or personal circumstances, jump-shooting sometimes provides the only alternative to bird watching in the field and spaghetti on the table. But stalking ducks doesn't receive much attention in the classical literature of American waterfowling, and little wonder: bellycrawling can never rival the grand pageant of birds settling into decoys at first light. I can't remember the last time I saw a work of sporting art depict a dog and hunter creeping through the mud toward a rafted flock of mallards. But despite this short shrift from the arbiters of taste, I suspect that jump-shooting accounts for more ducks every fall than more prestigious waterfowling methods, and it's hard to argue with success.

Spot-and-stalk tactics remain well suited to younger hunters for whom the impulse to take the chase to the game outweighs the subtler pleasures of waiting patiently beside a decoy spread. These days, I generally prefer the visual drama of decoying birds to the mercenary methods of the jump-shooter. I seldom set out to sneak a limit of ducks anymore except in certain well-defined circumstances, none of them more compelling than the need to put a duck dinner on the table.

A recent trip to the Rio Grande border country found my wife, Lori, and me bouncing down a mesquite-lined back road with our friend Ricardo Longoria after a long day of bowhunting. Ricardo's wife, Josephina, was due to join us at the ranch that evening and we wanted to celebrate her arrival with something special on the table. As we discussed our culinary options, we passed a little two-acre tank that held an assortment of ducks tucked up against the far shoreline. Since we were armed with nothing other than bows and arrows, the birds seemed safe, but Ricardo remembered that he had a pair of 20-gauge quail guns back at the hacienda. Fifteen minutes later, we set off into the dusk to give our plainly skeptical host an introduction to the fine art of jump- shooting.

With no high banks to disguise our approach, we had to circle through the brush to put some foliage between ourselves and our quarry, no easy task in country whose flora sport a world-class selection of thorns. After a hundred yards of jungle warfare, we tore our way through the final curtain of brush and flushed the birds against the sunset sky. The flock contained a splendid assortment of puddle ducks, and I deliberately picked out and dropped pintail, gadwall, and wigeon to provide some variety on the table. My only regret came from the lack of a dog, especially when I had to shuck off my shoes and swim for the downed birds floating on the pond. Classic waterfowling? Hardly, but no one complained, especially after we gnawed our way through a memorable meal of mesquite-grilled duck in orange sauce back at the hacienda that night.

Providing a young dog with valuable experience offers another great excuse for setting out on a midday jump-shoot. Blinds can be frustrating places for novice retrievers that have yet to develop the ability to sit still for long periods without fidgeting. Most young dogs would rather go jump-shooting than squirm in a blind for hours, awaiting deferred gratification from ducks that might or might not arrive. Jump-shooting works best as a training exercise when you have a hunting partner along to act as designated hitter, freeing you to concentrate on working—and controlling—the dog. From a tactical standpoint, creeks often serve the jump shooter's interests better than ponds and lakes, but it's best to avoid swift current when working a young dog, partly for safety reasons and partly because downstream turns out to be a remarkably difficult concept to teach most retrievers. So keep it simple. All you really want the youngster to learn is that following your commands will produce retrieves.

Jump-shooting demands the services of a capable water dog, and being able to play the game well should be part of any hunting retriever's job description. As usual, the most important element of training boils down to simple control, as anyone who has slimed their way through a hundred yards of mud only to have a jump blown by an undisciplined dog can attest. Since ducks hear better than most of us think, the approach to shotgun range must take place quietly, without benefit of shouts and whistles. After the command heel becomes an established part of the dog's vocabulary, practice it while you're crawling, just to let the dog know that the rules are the same whether you're standing in a blind or lying on your belly. The dog's profile may be a bit higher than yours, but that's seldom a practical problem as long as your canine companion will sit steadily a few yards behind you during the last few yards of the approach.

Of course, some dogs learn to crawl like predators themselves. Sky mastered this trick with minimal instruction, and by his third season, as soon as I'd hit the deck he'd start to slink along beside me like a coyote stalking a fawn. I'm not sure how many extra ducks his sneaking ability earned us over the years, but I do know how much I appreciated his company during the course of some of those long crawls. After all, wet mud always feels best when shared with a friend.

Winter has made the inside of the house so much more appealing than the landscape beyond the frosted windows that I have spent the morning holed up like a bear, tying flies and wrestling with deadlines that allow no consideration for the weather. And here I would remain except for an unexpected call for a duck dinner. We are expecting another couple for company tonight, and Lori has issued a polite but firm request for four prime mallards for the kitchen. Despite the inclement temperature outside, I have to admit that as household chores go, this one leaves little room to complain.

Do I take the old dog or the young one? Decisions, decisions. Standing alertly in his kennel outside, Jake certainly looks full of the youthful enthusiasm that ordinarily goes best with this kind of project, but as soon as the gun cabinet door opens, Sonny leaps up from the mat in front of the stove and seals the deal.

There is no question of setting up the decoys this afternoon, for the weather is just too awful. Bundled up against the worst of the wind chill, I invite the dog to join me in the pickup's front seat as I set off toward the creek with a single-minded purpose: to collect four greenheads and get back in front of the fire as soon as possible.

Fortunately, I know the water well enough to take most of the guesswork out of the hunt. Our late-season birds always favor certain bends in the creek where the current creates quiet backwaters to their liking, and over the years I've developed a route from one favorite place to the next that seems as familiar as the layout of a golf course. Sonny has never learned to crawl the way Sky did, but the high bank at our first approach makes that kind of stealth unnecessary. And sure enough, there are the mallards, two drakes and two hens, all flushing together the instant my silhouette violates their horizon. But not even their acute senses can save them today, and moments after the rise both drakes lie kicking in the snow on the opposite bank. Sonny frisks like a puppy as he emerges from the water on the far side of the creek, but after a quick romp he settles down to business and completes the job at hand.

The snow has drifted in along the edge of the field, and the trek downstream to the next jump nearly makes me long for snowshoes. One lone drake springs skyward as we top the bank, and for a moment I imagine having to bull my way through another half mile of snow in order to complete my mission. But at the sound of the shot, a familiar high-pitched whistle fills the air as a goldeneye flushes right beneath us and heads downstream just above the dancing water. After a quick safety check on the dog's position, I pivot about and fire, silencing the whistles and leaving a bundle of black and white feathers floating away down-stream on the current.

Because the stream is a spring creek, it never freezes and I don't have to worry about treacherous ice ledges down-stream. Consequently, I call Sonny off the stone-dead mal-lard and send him off toward the rapidly disappearing goldeneye. He spots the fallen bird just before it disappears around the next bend, and runs it down neatly, no small feat for a dog his age. Then it's back across the creek one last time for the mallard, and we're done.

There's ice on both my beard and Sonny's muzzle by the time we reach the truck. Despite the wet dog smell I know the heater will liberate, I let Sonny hop in the front seat with me, a minor privilege he has certainly earned. Although the final hours of the season lie fading away behind us as we turn up the hill toward home, it's hard to avoid a certain degree of con-tentment. Against all odds, the dog and I have found a simple way to celebrate its passage, and sometimes simplicity serves just as well as spectacle.

Chapter Three

HAIL COLUMBIA

B ack when I was a kid, Washington's Cascade Mountains formed a personal line of demarcation between civilization and wilderness. To the west lay school, traffic, noise, and obligation; to the east, mallards, chukar, silence, and freedom. The long drive across Snoqualamie Pass toward the sunrise felt like an act of liberation. David Guterson wrote his second novel about this very phenomenon, and despite the general critical impression of a sophomore slump, I read *East of the Mountains* with the special pleasure readers always reserve for books based in settings of intense personal significance.

My memories of hunting in Washington were nearly forty years old when Lori and I flew back to visit my parents last January. When my dad asked us to drive east of the mountains with him to hunt ducks on his property in the Columbia Basin, I really didn't know what to say. Thomas Wolfe once famously suggested that you can't go home

again, and as we loaded our gear and the dog into his truck I
wondered if my memories might not be better off left undisturbed. Attempting to recreate the best of one's childhood
can be a dangerous proposition, at least as likely to disap-
point as to enlighten. But I sensed that this was something
we needed to do, so with Lori between us in the front seat of
the truck, we waved goodbye to my mother and pulled out
of the driveway to see if we could prove Wolfe wrong.

We found the pass awash in a gloriously miserable brew
of fog and fresh, slushy snow. While the road conditions
hardly warranted mention by Montana standards, cars lined
the ditches, reminding us that we were sharing the highway
with thousands of weekend travelers unaccustomed to real
winter driving. Traffic slowed to a labored crawl by the
time we reached the summit, but when we passed the ski
runs the crowds began to thin. As we accelerated downward
through the clearing weather on the dry side of the
Cascades, it was hard to avoid the impression that we were
leaving a lot of distraction in our wake. In fact, the changes
reckoned over the years only emphasized the welcome sense
of departure from the urban sprawl behind us. Since my
childhood, Seattle had grown into a high-tech bastion of
smug political correctness, but ahead of us the Columbia
Basin looked pretty much the way I remembered it: windswept, austere, yet paradoxically appealing to the outdoorsman's heart.

Several years earlier, my parents had acquired an interest in a ranch property managed sensibly for waterfowl. Lori and I had never seen the place, and my father clearly seemed eager to show us around. As we drove down the road bordering the property, open water rose by magic from the background of sage and stubble, and right along with it ducks appeared overhead. Since I hadn't seen any waterfowl but spring creek mallards since freeze-up back home in Montana, their variety impressed me even more than their numbers. I've always been the kind of hunter who appreciates the pleasures of a mixed bag, and the sight of all those pintail, wigeon, and teal mixed in with the greenheads made me anticipate the next day's sunrise with special intensity.

We spent the rest of the afternoon visiting friends of my father's. Everyone seemed to have a copy of *The Life of a Lab* for me to sign. I tried to point out that I had merely provided a bit of verbal glue to hold Denver Bryan's superb photographs together on the pages, but no one seemed to care. When we finally retired to a motel in nearby Richland, I felt pleasantly exhausted, but I wasn't too tired to appreciate the eerie sense of déjà vu derived from finding myself in eastern Washington with my father again after all those years.

Washington residents claim that it never rains east of the mountains, but aridity can be relative by Seattle standards. A layer of wet scud obscured the moon as we unloaded our gear the following morning, and by the time we began to set out the decoys, the dampness in the air had turned to freezing drizzle. But no one appreciates the hidden pleasures of foul weather like a duck hunter, and the sound of wings whistling through the gloom overhead quickly eased the chill. The blind proved spacious enough to accommodate all three of us and my father's Lab, and as we settled in I had difficulty imagining a better place to await the sunrise.

Time seldom passes as slowly as it does just before legal shooting light. A pair of mallards slid in low above the blocks, but the minute hand on my watch had not yet reached the necessary position on the dial and we let them pass. Just as the appointed moment crept round at last, a half dozen birds appeared with their wings set against the gradually freshening light. "Let's do it," Dad whispered, and we pivoted into position to take them.

As we rose to our feet, I studied the flaring birds and identified the distinctive tuxedo markings of a mature drake pintail. "Just one apiece!" I cried into the rain, and then I felt the wet stock against my cheek and watched the bird I had been tracking shudder and collapse at the sound of the shot. My father had killed a bird as well, and as the ejectors spit the empty shells into our hands we paused and studied our day's limit of sprig bobbing in the decoys.

Pintail numbers had been down for several years in the Central Flyway, and two full seasons had passed since I last killed one. The sight of abundant pintails in the air the day before made me start thinking about killing a well-plumaged drake to mount, but as the dog delivered the first bird to my father's hand, I realized the specimen really wasn't of presentation quality. Nonetheless, the species has always held a special spot in my heart, and I appreciated the opportunity to hunt an area where they were abundant enough to let me feel good about killing one. For a moment, I remembered the old days when pintails were worth a dime in a hundred-point limit, but a lot had changed since then. Now the law said one was enough for each of us, and the law had it right.

We barely had time to reload before a lone greenwing appeared, flitting down out of the heavy sky like a jet-powered moth, as only teal can fly. I deferred to my father who in turn deferred to me. By the time we finished this Alphonse and Gaston routine, the bird had nearly climbed back out of range, but I wanted to kill a teal and I stood up and dropped it. The bird fell into the grass along the far waterline, and suddenly it was time for the dog to prove her worth.

A six-year-old yellow Lab, Goldie had been my fiftieth anniversary present to my parents. Despite her origins in my own kennel, the dog and I had never really managed to make friends. My folks loved her though, and I knew Dad wanted her to perform well for our benefit. Instead, she proved my own personal Law of the Bird Dog: They always save the worst for the times their handlers want them to act their best. The good news is that she found the teal; the bad news is better left to the imagination. Let's just agree to call the retrieve a success and leave its description at that.

With three quick birds resting on the bench beside us, we settled back to do what waterfowlers do best: wait. Although half an hour passed before we next saw a duck in range, it would be hard to accuse the time of passing slowly. Birds appeared overhead constantly, giving us an opportunity to call and discuss their identity. When a small flock of mallards finally set their wings and dropped in to visit, the shooting that followed came almost as an afterthought. As the birds hung over the decoys, I concentrated on separating drakes from hens, and when we were through, Goldie quickly capitalized on the opportunity we had provided for her redemption.

Uncharacteristically, Dad missed twice on that set of birds. When I was growing up, I regarded him as the best wingshot I'd ever seen. While many young hunters enjoy the same opinion of their fathers, few get to see it confirmed by the passage of time and the endorsement of their peers. I was one of the lucky ones. But while my father had approached the age of eighty with uncommon grace, he had also suffered a small stroke the previous September. Despite his gratifying recovery, I still noticed minor coordination flaws that might have escaped the attention of even the most astute clinical observer. It wasn't that he couldn't shoot anymore. He just seemed to hesitate when it came time to stand and take a bird on the wing, a process sometimes difficult enough for the young. But he had also developed an even more uncommon skill: the ability to adjust his attitude to his own recent shortcomings. He was killing less but enjoying the process as much as always, and his dignity demanded my admiration as much as the remarkable shooting ability I had known in years gone by.

We never experienced a torrent of birds in the decoys that morning. But there were always ducks visible somewhere, and the constant activity in the air and the comfort of the blind made the hours pass as easily as water flowing downstream. A flight of teal zoomed in low over the brush behind us, offering us a chance to embarrass ourselves with our first shots before we settled down and killed a pair with our second. Mallards trickled in one and two at a time. We passed on the hens but added several more drakes to the growing collection on the bench. Pintails appeared regularly, and while we couldn't shoot any more, there was no prohibition against enjoying the aerial display they put on overhead as they approached the decoys. Finally, I heard the high-pitched cry of a wigeon somewhere behind us, and when a lone drake appeared with its wings set, I rose and killed him, and without discussion we all agreed that we were done.

As always, collecting the decoys aroused a detached feeling of anticlimax, like taking down the Christmas tree or starting to work on the dishes after the last of the company has gone. Of course, several flocks of birds tried to land on my head as I forged unarmed through the muck with the decoy bag, but I expected as much and felt too philosophical to regret our decision to call it a day. Lori tried to get Dad to let us carry all the gear back to the truck, but he wouldn't hear of it. The three of us slogged side by side toward dry land beneath the load of guns, decoys, and ducks, while Goldie romped eagerly through the swamp, enjoying her last measure of freedom before the long ride home.

Dad took the first shift behind the wheel as we started down the highway. The drive's hypnotic pace and the glorious miles of nothing soon made me drowsy. As I leaned against Lori and drifted off to sleep, I remembered a whole childhood's worth of Sunday-night drives west toward home. I didn't even have a driver's license back in those days, and there was nothing to worry about except the next day's schoolwork. But the hum of the truck and my father's reassuring presence always made me feel wonderfully secure and it still did, even after all the years and all the miles that had passed since then. All that nostalgia went right over Lori's head, but I think Dad felt it too, and it became a secret for the two of us to share as we crossed the river and began to climb slowly through the foothills of the Cascades.

Snow was falling in the pass again as we started into the backstretch of the long drive home. As always, the transition from the open terrain on the eastern side of the Cascades to

the towering conifers to the west felt shockingly abrupt. As we wound our way down out of the mountains, the traffic seemed to swell at every freeway entrance, like water joining a river on its way to the sea. The feel of Seattle gathering itself around us as we drove reminded me of all I had given up when I left the city for the wilds of Montana and Alaska three decades before. But it also reminded me of the reasons for my choice, and in the end I felt no regrets.

We cooked the ducks for family and friends at my parents' house that night. Although she cooks game well, my mother has always been oddly uncomfortable with waterfowl, so I showed her how I prefer to manage prime specimens: hot and quick, with a minimum of hocus-pocus. The blood-rare ducks this method produces aren't for everyone, and I'll admit to a bit of anxiety as I placed the platter on the table. But before we were through, everyone was slurping at the bones like a pack of hungry carnivores, and whatever thoughts I might have entertained about saving a teal for breakfast vanished right along with the second bottle of wine.

And that's pretty much the way it should have ended. Hunts fix themselves in the memory for a variety of reasons: spectacular physical settings, exceptional dog work, occasionally furious shooting. While this simple expedition boasted no such excitement, it served an even higher purpose. By the time Lori and I left for Montana, I knew all over again where I had come from and why. The mechanism of this realization came courtesy of a few simple tools: a gun, a dog, the right people, and the ducks.

Together, we had proved Wolfe wrong, and I for one felt glad.

Chapter Four

CHILD'S PLAY

The memories of my first duck hunt—still remarkably vivid even after more years than I care to count—owe a surprising debt to my sense of smell.

That's a strange observation, since waterfowling is a profoundly visual experience, full of dramatic sunrises and sunsets and the intricately choreographed spectacle of ducks on the wing circling decoys in tantalizing spirals. Few activities in outdoor sport lend themselves so well to representational artwork, as decades worth of duck stamps and DU prints readily demonstrate. And what the eyes reveal, the ears embellish, from the seductive plaint of a duck call to a shotgun's dramatic bark at the moment of truth. Nonetheless, the most memorable impressions of that long-ago morning somehow imprinted themselves through my nose.

It started in the kitchen, with nothing but darkness visible beyond the windows and an all but uncontainable sense of excitement in the air. A child among men, I was lucky to have been asked along, and I knew it. As my father's friends arrived and gathered about the breakfast table, I sat quietly inside a vastly outsized set of woolens and toyed with an egg over easy while the dog skittered about the linoleum floor and the grownups talked strategy in terms utterly meaningless to me at the time. And what I remember is the smell of the coffee, rich and bitter yet oddly invigorating, even though I was still too young to know what morning coffee really meant. Surely I had smelled that smell before, but it left no impression until then.

The drive through the darkness to the lake seemed interminable. My father, clad in waders, had to carry me from the shore to the blind, and I remember the smell of the pipe smoke on his jacket as I buried my face against his shoulder and tried not to think about the dark, frigid lake water slipping past beneath. Once inside the blind, I sat on the bench and clung to the dog—a well-mannered shorthair named Bits—while my father and his friends dropped the decoys in circles about the blind. Somehow, the wet dog smell seemed to ward off the loneliness of that temporary abandonment.

The sun finally crept above the horizon, but I remember almost nothing about that first duck blind sunrise. My father had cautioned me against spooking ducks by looking up, and I took his advice to heart, fixing my gaze so relentlessly on the mud underfoot that my memory of the next hour consists of little but monochromatic gloom. But suddenly I heard nervous whispers on either side, and the grownups rose and shot, and when Bits returned to the blind he carried with him a dead black duck whose rich organic aroma captivated me as I held it in my lap and guarded it like some plumed treasure. I was too young to understand the subtleties of what had taken place, but I knew that I never wanted to be left out and that I wanted to return again and again.

Thanks to understanding parents, I managed to fulfill that wish.

We lived in upstate New York back then, hardly a water-fowling hotspot by any stretch of the imagination. But despite their dependence on wetland habitat, ducks offer the most widely distributed wingshooting opportunities in North America: give them open water and they will come. And because I was young and enthusiastic, it didn't take a lot of ducks to keep me happy. Any outing that resulted in a dead duck felt like a good day, and we regarded a morning in a blind that produced a couple of flocks in range as a triumph. The shooting couldn't begin to match what we encountered when my family moved to Washington when I was in high school, much less the Central Flyway action I discovered in eastern Montana ten years later. But I was fortunate enough to make this pilgrim's progress in the right direction, with each new venue offering excitement above and beyond the last. Since I didn't know any better at the time, the beaver ponds and backwaters I hunted as kid offered a perfectly serviceable introduction to the pleasures of waterfowling.

The ducks we hunted lacked in variety just as surely as they lacked for numbers, but we made up for those deficiencies in the quality of the species we shot. Woodies were our go-to ducks and they probably accounted for three-fourths of all the waterfowl I killed while I was growing up. We drifted down on them in our canoe and jumped them along the edges of winding creeks, and I still remember the tight little formations they flew in and their striking appearance when Bits delivered them to my hand. Now that I hardly ever get to see a wood duck anymore, I feel real heaviness in my heart when I think about all the drakes I plucked casually, without saving one for the taxidermist. Why do we so often fail to appreciate natural beauty until we've lost the opportunity to enjoy it.

Setting out decoys on larger water meant matching wits with black ducks, an opportunity I'd love to reenact now that I have decades more waterfowling experience under my belt. Were they really that smart or was I just that inexperienced? I'll never be certain, but I do know that when Bits arrived back in the blind with a mouthful of black duck, the sight evoked the kind of satisfaction ordinarily reserved for big game. Wary black ducks taught me all kinds of valuable lessons about duck blind comportment, and it didn't take a lot of dead ones at the end of the morning to make me feel like a hunter.

In a sense, waterfowl always provided something of a sidelight during my formative years. We did live near good grouse and woodcock cover. Bits was a superb upland dog, and my father, who knew a bit more of the wingshooting life than I did, obviously preferred fast upland action to mediocre waterfowling, especially in the company of a once-in-a-lifetime grouse dog. While I certainly spent my share of time tramping through alders, beeches, and abandoned apple orchards in search of grouse, duck hunting cast a spell on me right from the beginning, meager as the shooting itself usually proved back in those early days. I loved the excitement of rising in the dark, the production of the decoy spread, and the tantalizing drama of birds circling through the air. I also acquired an early taste for ducks on the table, providing an extra measure of satisfaction from every instance of success.

Duck hunting also taught me lasting lessons about the relationship between hunters and dogs in the field. Because of my father's dedication to grouse hunting, we stuck with shorthairs back then, but Bits proved to be both a capable water dog and an enjoyable companion during our waterfowl excursions. When we hunted upland game, we hardly even saw him except when his bell stopped tinkling down in the cover and we moved in to locate the point. But when we hunted ducks, he was always there at my side, enforcing my early enthusiasm for canine company. My long eventual relationship with Labrador retrievers no doubt evolved from after-school duck hunts decades ago, when I usually saw a lot more of the dog than the ducks.

Those early experiences also left me with a firm appreciation for the appeal of wetland habitat. With a splendid mantle of autumn foliage, the upland cover we hunted then hardly lacked for charm. Nonetheless, I always felt myself mysteriously drawn to the creeks and marshes where we hunted ducks. An enthusiastic amateur naturalist right from the start, I enjoyed the opportunity they afforded to observe a variety of incidental wildlife, from wading birds to furbearers. At an early age, I learned that ducks frequented interesting places, and the ability to appreciate my surroundings as I waited for their arrival helped compensate for those occasions when they chose not to appear at all.

Once I matured enough to carry a shotgun of my own in the field, I quickly developed a special regard for ducks on the wing. I shot grouse and woodcock fairly well for my age, but the shooting consisted mostly of blurs and bangs, and its challenge derived for the most part from being able to identify a target against a complex visual background and track it quickly before it disappeared in the trees. Waterfowl, on the other hand, offered tantalizing visual anticipation followed by snappy angles and the chance to watch the result of a successful shot plummet lazily toward the water below. The whole process felt immensely satisfying, and I soon found myself willing to endure long hours in the cold just for a chance to enjoy it.

When describing those formative childhood experiences to friends, especially those who never hunted themselves, I've had more than one tell me I must have been crazy. Possibly, but I see things in a different light. I think I must have been lucky as hell.

Lean as the shooting itself sometimes proved, my early waterfowling experiences weren't all long days and empty skies. Real excitement lay buried among the long hours of watching and waiting, and I can remember some of it as clearly as if it took place yesterday.

One November afternoon, my father and I concluded a long day in the upland cover by driving to a nearby creek bottom to wait out the last hour of light over a decoy spread. Beavers had flooded a stand of alders, and we dropped a dozen blocks in the black water and settled down on the bank to wait. I think my father would have preferred to head for home, a hot bath, and a glass of bourbon, but he knew where my heart lay by then. Besides, Bits was on my side, and according to the splendid principles of democracy enjoyed by men and boys and dogs, we had him outvoted.

As usual, not much happened for some time. Eventually, a lone greenwing rocketed down out of the snow-laden sky, and my father allowed me the honor of missing it twice before he dropped it at the far edge of shot-gun range. My misses didn't bother me in the least. I got to watch the dog hit the water in a glorious geyser of spray, and when he returned, the teal was mine to hold and examine in the waning light. That was enough back then, just as it should have been.

Real gloom finally began to gather. We had unloaded and gathered in the decoys when a high-pitched whistling noise suddenly rose from the darkness overhead. While its source remained invisible at first, the noise grew relentlessly in volume until I practically had to shout to make myself heard. The racket reminded me of a jet engine spooling up for takeoff (a sound I'd only heard a time or two myself back then), and since this hunt took place during a period of peak Cold War nuclear jitters, I seriously wondered if we were under some kind of attack. "What is it?" I cried as I instinctively gathered Bits to my side for protection.

"Ducks!" my father answered. "My God, Donnie! Look at the ducks!" Then I saw them at last, a swirling vortex of mallards and black ducks rotating downward out of the sky like a tornado, all furiously intent on landing in the half-acre puddle we'd temporarily claimed as our own. Instinctively, I rose to my feet and tried to isolate a target from the chaos overhead, but paternal wisdom prevailed. "It's too dark to shoot, and this is something special," my father advised over the racket. "Let's just watch and listen."

And we did. As the vast flocked side-slipped downward toward the little beaver pond, the noise of cold air whistling through extended primaries slowly yielded to the warm, contented chuckle of ducks on the water. The temperature seemed to rise from the proximity of their body heat, as if we'd all found ourselves together in a cabin somewhere. When we finally stood and shouldered the decoy bags to begin the hike back to the road, a few of the nearest birds offered brief alarm cries, but the presence of so much company quickly reassured them. By the time we reached the edge of the nearby field, the little pond and its occupants seemed as undisturbed as if we'd never been there. "Do you see why I didn't want to shoot?" my father asked, and it sounded as if he were offering an apology.

"Yes," I told him, and I meant it. I've experienced similar breathtaking late-evening arrivals several times since then, and each time I've broken my gun and watched and listened, even when enough light remained to finish out a limit legally. Lots of parents teach their kids to shoot, but it takes special wisdom to teach them that you don't always have to.

Lucky, not crazy. I knew it all the time.

In the years since then, I've hunted waterfowl from Alaska to Mexico, in all four of the continent's major flyways. Waterfowl have been good to me, and I've enjoyed plenty of the kind of furious shooting writers love to go on about in print. But I've always stood firm in my conviction that the pace of the shooting and the heft of the bag at the end of the day have remarkably little bearing on the overall value of the experience. Perhaps hunts are best measured by the endurance of the memories they produce, in which case I've made remarkably little progress since those early days, when duck hunting consisted largely of patience and hope. Black ducks and woodies, long, fruitless scans across lonely skies, a wise teacher, and a devoted dog...sometimes I wonder if it's possible to have it any better.

Chapter Five

SNOW STORM

The story begins in the heart of the central Canadian Arctic tundra, as splendidly remote an expanse of wilderness as any left on earth. You can still fly this country for hours at low altitude without seeing signs of human intrusion. Between the autumnal and vernal equinoxes, snow and ice encase the terrain, limiting its occupancy to a select list of hardy, cold-adapted survivors: caribou, arctic foxes, ptarmigan, snowy owls, polar bears. But the sun's inevitable return each spring magically converts this apparent wasteland into its ecological opposite as ice melts and vast, fertile wetlands form in its place, providing an undisturbed summer breeding ground for a diverse assortment of our continent's shorebirds and waterfowl.

Some hunters may not care much about curlews and plovers and such, a loss for all concerned, especially the hunters themselves. Personally, I've never been able to divorce my enthusiasm for any quarry from an appreciation

47

of the habitat it occupies and the company it keeps. Regardless of where one falls on this ideological spectrum, the central Canadian Arctic plain deserves respect for its reliable contributions to North America's annual fall flight of waterfowl. And of all the diverse species of ducks and geese that call the tundra their summer home, none is more numerically important than *Anser c. caerulescens*, the lesser snow goose.

The tundra has experienced a potentially dangerous embarrassment of riches over the last decade, as snow goose numbers exploded from the area's historic carrying capacity of a million and a half birds to a population four times that size. While the diminutive little snow goose may seem an unlikely agent of ecological destruction, nature pays a price for an excess of anything. Despite its isolation and imposingly harsh appearance, the Arctic tundra turns out to be remarkably fragile habitat. As all those geese relentlessly attacked the forbs and grasses that renew the food chain every spring, they laid waste to the countryside, eventually threatening not only their own survival but the future of dozens of other waterbird species as well.

Our Fish and Wildlife Service responded to the gathering crisis by encouraging the harvest of snow geese through a variety of regulatory mechanisms: extending seasons, eliminating bag limits, and liberalizing means of take. In the politically charged atmosphere that complicates modern wildlife management, such measures predictably aroused their share of controversy. I'll admit to a certain ambivalence myself, especially after a decade of drought and limited waterfowl production during which I voluntarily chose to limit my own take in the field.

But finally curiosity and an appreciation of biologic reality overcame my inhibitions. Since Montana doesn't offer a lot of snow goose hunting opportunities and did not choose to exercise the option of spring seasons and generous limits, that meant traveling. In March of 1999 I set off for the plains of eastern Colorado to find out what the fuss was all about.

As a longtime resident of eastern Montana, I enjoy a long familiarity with big skies. But as the sun crept slowly over the distant edge of the horizon, the size of the space overhead practically took my breath away. The sky didn't just look big there; it looked immense. Vast brown fields of corn stalks and wheat stubble formed a gigantic checkerboard all the way to the nearby Kansas border. Barely visible in the early light, a serpentine line of cottonwoods marked the course of the Arkansas River bottom, home to some of the country's least-appreciated big whitetails. But as I braced myself against the brisk morning air, I felt preoccupied by matters more immediate than scenery or antlers, for it was early March, and we were hunting snow geese, a venture that seemed to be growing to epic proportions right before my eyes.

Despite a lifetime afield in the north, I approached the morning's hunt as a relative novice. My Montana home lies on the cusp between the Central and Pacific flyways, and migrating snows pass far to either side. Back when I lived in Alaska, huge flights of snow geese visited the mouth of the nearby Kenai River every spring, but they overflew Cook Inlet during hunting season. The bottom line was that a good dog could retrieve every snow I'd ever shot in less time than it takes to tell.

Fortunately, my friends John Eden and Jeff Travis more than compensated for my own lack of experience. They live and breathe geese from late October until it's time to stop hunting, which in these strange times doesn't take place until basketball playoffs are in progress and wild turkeys have started to strut. And after all those mornings spent lying in the stubble, they realized full well that a successful snow goose hunt begins with an industrial-strength decoy spread.

The object, John had explained an hour earlier when we exited his vehicle in the dark, was to make the field look white. It took me a while to realize that he meant acres of the field. In fact, the contents of Jeff's Suburban could have stocked an American Museum of Snow Goose Decoys, including everything from magnum shells to fliers, silhouettes, and gunny sacks full of rags that I had been assigned to plant along the edges of the corn stalks. Needless to say, we were not setting out dozens of decoys but hundreds, and

by the time dawn broke at last I could finally appreciate just what an immense artificial spread we had created.

"Geese!" Jeff suddenly cried as he straightened from the last of the silhouettes and raised a hand for silence. The breeze had barely risen enough to add a breath of life to the rag decoys, and as I concentrated on the aural blankness of the calm sky overhead I finally appreciated the distant, high-pitched ululation of snows on the wing. The birds were still too far off to see, but the racket confirmed that they had lifted off a distant reservoir and started for the fields to feed. All we could do now was hope that the host of white artifacts scattered across the barren ground would coax them into range.

As we scrambled toward the downwind edge of the decoys, I found myself overcome by doubt. Our plans for concealment seemed remarkably primitive in comparison to our elaborate decoy spread. At John's urging, I simply lay supine in a furrow at the edge of the cut corn stalks and pulled a white sheet over my legs. I found it hard to believe this minimalist approach to goose blinds would fool much of anything despite my hosts' reassurances to the contrary. But these guys knew their snow geese, I reminded myself as I settled into the soft dirt to wait, and I didn't.

When the first line of geese finally appeared far off in the sky, my confidence sank as rapidly as my excitement rose. The country around us looked big enough to swallow every goose in the flyway, and nothing but the spread of rags and shells distinguished our lonely field from all the rest. But John still had a trick or two up his sleeve. At the first sight of birds headed in our direction, he began to play a goose-shaped kite upward into the breeze with an old fiberglass fly rod. Then he began to call, and as we all

joined in, a chorus of goose talk rose from our decoy spread. Shortly thereafter, the first flock began to veer in our direction and lose altitude.

Never mind the possibility of shooting to follow; the sheer spectacle of the birds' approach justified all the effort we had invested in their attraction. Flying in a disorganized, undulating formation, the geese began to gather themselves in waves. Their plumage caught the early-morning light high overhead and broadcast it like a beacon: a long string of pearls torn and spilled across the cerulean blue sky. As the leading edge of the flock began to side-slip downward along an imaginary glide path, I suddenly realized that the birds were about to cross the threshold into shotgun range.

Accustomed to wary honkers back home, I remained frozen to the ground until the birds were right overhead, an unnecessary exercise in discipline as I would learn over the course of the long morning. Demonstrating herd mentality at its worst, the snows seemed to make decisions by committee, and once they decided to investigate our spread it became practically impossible to deter them. Finally, I rose to my knees, concentrated on picking one bird from the flock, and fired. I was shooting a borrowed 10-gauge, but the heavy gun seemed to lock onto its target naturally, and as I pulled away and slapped the trigger, the bird crumbled and fell from the sky with such operatic grandeur that I forgot about the second barrel entirely.

By Dawn's Early Light

While watching a thousand geese approach at once can be a spectacular experience, most seasoned hunters would prefer to have a fraction of that number set their wings overhead in staggered flights of ten or twenty, which is exactly what happened over the course of the next two hours. With the largest flocks already committed to the fields of their choice, we were shooting stragglers, but the smaller groups of birds decoyed eagerly. While none of the little flocks actually put their landing gear down, most provided us with elegant overhead passing shots, which is all any reasonable gunner has the right to ask. We missed a few and killed plenty more, and by the time we decided to stand up and begin the laborious task of collecting all those decoys, I felt as satisfied and full as if I had just finished a long meal at a favorite restaurant.

Early the following morning, we set out for another field with a new mission. This time, I meant to test myself against the geese with an entirely different weapon: my recurve bow. When the first set of snows materialized just after sunrise, I picked the lowest bird, drew on it just as I would have with a shotgun, doubled my lead, and watched my arrow sail harmlessly through the air behind my target. Six sets of geese later, I hadn't cut a feather, although the stubble field in front of us sprouted white-fletched flu-flu arrows like spring daisies. As an unrepentant advocate of the bow, admitting failure did not come easily. Nonetheless, I finally had to acknowledge that I had chosen the wrong tool for the job.

"Hey, Jeff!" I called across the stubble as yet another line of birds appeared on the horizon. "Mind if I borrow a shotgun?" He didn't, and when a single peeled away from the next flock and floated toward our spread, I rose to one knee and dropped it like a stone. As I fed another shell into the magazine, I experienced a moment of regret, for that was the closest bird I had seen all morning and it would have provided my best opportunity yet for the bow. But as is usually the case with geese, the range had been farther than appearances suggested. Only when I paced off the distance to the limp white form did I realize that the bird had been thirty-five yards away when I killed it. Since that's a challenging shot for a bow even when the target isn't moving as fast as a truck cruising down a dirt road, I felt some vindication for my earlier string of misses.

By the time we finished for the morning, vast, noisy flocks of snows had started to descend from dizzying heights toward a nearby reservoir. These were new arrivals in the area, according to John, since local residents didn't fly that high when traveling to and from the fields. As surely as the next sunrise, the annual northward migration had begun. But to what would these birds return when they finally reached their destination? Just how much abuse can one species inflict upon a fragile ecosystem before things fall apart, as Yeats suggested, and the center no longer holds? Despite the obvious irony of a species as destructive as our own asking this question of one as fundamentally benign as the snow goose, I found it hard not to consider the problem even as I enjoyed the bounty it has temporarily created. In the meantime, as the geese and I readied for our own northward journeys, I drew some consolation from the thought with which I end every hunting season: There would always be next year.

Let's hope.

Chapter Six

MILLENNIUM MALLARDS

On the morning of January 1, 2000, I rose at a leisurely hour, let Sonny out the kitchen door, and paused to watch the sun break over the hills on the eastern horizon just as I had known it would all along. I was not suffering from any indiscretions. In a rare concession to common sense, Lori and I had retired early the night before to let others party and fret about uncertainties in cyberspace. When Sonny returned from his morning tour of the yard, I reached for a light switch and turned it on, confirming the absence of electrical disaster. Then I walked upstairs, booted up the computer, and stared at the same collection of unfinished projects and tardy deadlines I had put to bed the night before. Finally I breathed a smug *I told you so* and prepared to do exactly what I would have done had civilization collapsed overnight: go duck hunting.

Setting out decoys midmorning runs counter to established waterfowling tradition, but our late start did not reflect laziness. Access to the place we planned to hunt required a drive right past the landowner's house, and even though he has assured me many times that early-morning arrivals don't bother him, I always feel bad about the idea of disturbing his hard-earned rest. So the sun stood high in the clear winter sky as Lori and I unloaded our gear and started toward the bend in the river where the mallards had been landing earlier in the week, but I didn't care. While most people were downing aspirin and settling in for a day of tele- vised football, we were outdoors getting ready to hunt, and it was hard to avoid feeling like the luckiest guy in the county.

To his obvious displeasure, we had left Sonny at home. He really started to show his age this season, and on our last duck hunt together I'd noticed him having some difficulty with the current and the icy banks along the river. While I found the idea of declaring him officially retired hard to accept, I certainly didn't enjoy watching him struggle to make retrieves he could have made in his sleep a few years earlier. And so we began the new year hunting with Jake, Sonny's opposite number both physically and mentally: long on strength and endurance, short on patience and wisdom. I suspected we might not enjoy his company quite as much, but I also realized the time had come to ring in the new in the kennel as well as on the calendar. Needless to say, no one demonstrated more enthusiasm for this changing of the guard than Jake himself.

Late-season duck shooting over small water doesn't require much in the way of decoys or blinds. After tossing out a dozen blocks, we settled into place beside a clump of brush, with the bank behind us to break up our outline. The air felt unseasonably pleasant from the start, and as the sun warmed the rocks around us we began to relax until it was hard to imagine we were hunting ducks on the high plains in January. While she can demonstrate remarkable discipline when it comes to ambushing whitetails with her bow, Lori has always tended toward impatience in duck blinds. But the weather felt so balmy that time passed as easily as the current in the river, and not even the young dog's fidgeting could compromise the pleasure of the day.

Then the whistle of wings overhead roused us from the languid flow of conversation. Startled, I mistimed my rise and found myself staring at a lone mallard drake flaring at the

edge of shotgun range. But when I shouldered the gun and slapped the trigger, the bird tumbled down out of the sky and crashed into the brush on the opposite bank. Lori wanted to see Jake do well even more than I did. When I released him, he hit the water with an enthusiastic splash, and moments later we were admiring the first bird of the New Year.

Twenty minutes later, a half dozen mallards suddenly appeared over the decoys. While Lori raised the camera, I picked two drakes from the flock and watched them tumble as I shot. The first collapsed stone dead in the decoy spread, but the second set its wings and sailed into a tangle of brush behind us, affording Jake his first challenging retrieve of the day. Mission accomplished, we dodged a shower of dog water and settled into our hiding place once more.

After missing a pass-shot at a single, I dropped a lone drake and watched the dog make another competent if unspectacular retrieve. With guests expected for dinner that night, Lori began to agitate for an early return home, but I was in the mood to complete a limit. Nearly an hour passed before we saw another bird. When the next pair dropped into the river one bend short of our decoy spread, I hiked down the bank and jumped them and that was that. I encouraged Lori to trade the camera for the shotgun, but she freely admitted that she was more interested in the hot tub back home than a bruising from my 12-gauge and five more ducks to pluck. With a pleasant morning's shoot and a limit's worth of gratifying dog work behind us, we elected to declare victory and withdraw.

We had enjoyed no grand spectacle, but we had accomplished what we came for, and on the first morning of the new century, that was enough.

I planned to spend the following morning hunting mountain lions in the hills above the house. But the warm weather had left poor tracking snow, and when my neighbor Rick Taylor called and asked if I wanted to join him and mutual friend Gene Miller at their duck pond instead, the invitation sounded like an offer I couldn't refuse. With three people in one blind, Rick politely suggested that we leave the retrieving duties to his experienced Lab, Jazz, and I took the hint. That meant two unhappy dogs at my house instead of one when I pulled out of the driveway in the dark, but that was their problem. I was going hunting even if they weren't.

Light snow and a low ceiling obscured the sky as we set out an ambitious decoy spread in the dull early-morning light. The temperature had dropped considerably overnight, and as we worked we did our best to convince ourselves that the wintry weather would surely translate into a morning's worth of fast shooting. Since the spring-fed pond offered the only open water around, there was some basis for that opinion, although most of this enforced optimism came for the benefit of the chilled feet that wound up in the blind once we'd set the last of the decoys. Finally, after consultation with our watches, we declared legal shooting light at hand and settled down to shiver and to wait.

Buoyed by coffee and conversation, the first hour passed uneventfully. But the colder the weather, the shorter the time to impatience on slow mornings in a duck blind, and by nine o'clock we were groping for explanations. "They're all still out in the fields, feeding," Gene suggested helpfully.

"The cold weather always makes them feed longer," Rick observed.

For my own part, I couldn't ignore the irony. The day before, on a mediocre piece of water, I'd killed a limit of birds while curled up next to a bush in the middle of a bluebird day. Now, under ideal conditions, in a well-constructed blind surrounded by fifty decoys, the sky overhead remained stubbornly empty. But hope springs eternal in the waterfowler's breast as in no other, and with cheerful company on either side and Jazz minding his manners beneath the bench, there really wasn't much to do but see the morning through to its conclusion.

Suddenly, a lone drake mallard appeared from nowhere and sailed past the decoy spread. We had not discussed shooting protocol in advance. As usual under such circumstances, we were all so busy deferring politely to each other that the bird nearly survived the last mistake of his life. Finally, I decided that courtesy has its limits, rose, and missed...with two witnesses to boot. Fortunately, I concentrated with my second barrel and dropped the bird in time to end my embarrassment.

Jazz was midway through the retrieve when Gene uttered a sudden cry that conveyed enough excitement to bring us all to our feet. For one glorious moment we stood and stared at the mallards wheeling overhead, and then we settled down to the production of order out of chaos, separating hens from drakes and avoiding birds that logically belonged to someone else. When the shooting was over, no one's feet felt cold anymore, and Jazz had become a pleasantly busy boy.

The dog work would have been routine except for a sheet of unreliable ice that stretched across the side of the pond opposite the spring behind us. We did our best to drop the birds short, but one long cripple made it to the shelf and waddled away toward the frozen reeds on the far bank. Jazz looked willing, but we didn't want to risk having him break through the ice. While Rick worked him on the birds lying safely on the water, I walked around the pond and picked up the duck's tracks in the freshly fallen snow. The webbed footprints led to an overhanging bank, but even on hands and knees I couldn't locate the bird. Finally Rick led the dog around the pond and turned him loose. He quickly sniffed out the duck and ran it down in the grass, proving all over again how craftily a downed mallard can act and how essential an experienced canine nose can be to its recovery.

With all the birds accounted for, we scrambled back into the blind just in time to receive the next set. The flock of forty came side-slipping down in waves, and once again it seemed easier to stare than to make the commitment to stand and shoot. Finally, I realized that we had all the birds we could handle in range, and when I yelled to take them we all rose in unison and did just that. We missed a couple but we dropped a whole lot more, and as Jazz went back to work again we broke our guns and stepped outside the blind to enjoy the show and recover from the excitement of shooting's furious pace.

It felt strange not to be handling one of my own dogs, but I gradually settled into the role of observer. Jazz took care of business in workmanlike fashion, without embellishment but without any mistakes, either. The birds he delivered all turned out to be prime northern mallards: orange-footed, long-billed, crops stuffed tight with grain from the nearby stubble fields. Those qualities can be difficult to appreciate when viewed down the end of a shotgun barrel, but in the hand, ducks like that convey a sense of quality and the promise of culinary rewards to come. By the time the dog had finished, we hadn't lost a bird and a head count confirmed that we were just two ducks shy of a limit.

Rick and I unloaded our guns, and he concentrated on the dog while I broke out the camera. Gene dropped two singles over the next thirty minutes. As we prepared to start picking up the blocks, one final, glorious flock of a hundred birds came winging in from the south, and the fact that there was no more shooting to be done only heightened our appreciation of their aerial display. When the birds finally spooked and flared and the cold gray sky lay empty once again above our heads, there was simply nothing left to be said, and we didn't even bother to try.

The temperature has continued to drop since Sunday, reminding us all over again what normal winters in Montana are supposed to feel like. This is the season when indoor spaces feel most inviting, when walls become less confining, and the cheer of warm fireplaces and good company makes up for all sorts of difficulty outside. The ducks we shot this weekend lie marinating in the refrigerator as I write. Tomorrow, everyone is coming over for dinner. I know just what's on the menu, and imagining the smell of roast duck permeating the house is enough to make me want to skip work for a morning and do it all over again.

The hunting I enjoyed over the last two days seems as remarkable for its differences as for its similarities. The trip to the river with Lori and Jake felt personal and intimate, fundamentally a family outing that happened to be punctuated by ducks. The morning in the blind by the pond, on the other hand, offered all the pageantry of classical waterfowling in the grand tradition. The fact that both outings ended with identical bags of five mallards each simply demonstrates the futility of reducing the outdoor experience to a matter of score.

Time magazine just declared Albert Einstein its Man of the Century, and it's hard to argue with the choice. But amid all the fin-de-siécle hoopla, it's disappointing not to hear more about ducks. After all, more than a hundred million of them made their way down the flyways this year, and a century that produced as much war and misery as the last should be able to take time to celebrate its successes. The ducks that so recently inspired and amazed us weren't there by accident. They were the product of commitment, foresight, and hard work, and the least I can do is express my appreciation.

Sonny is snuffling around happily beneath my desk as I write, last weekend's slight apparently forgiven. I'd like to take the old campaigner out one last time and I'm already performing the necessary mental gymnastics with the week's work schedule. His puppyhood seems like yesterday, but years sometimes pass as quickly as dawn's early light, and soon it will be time to move on. This may have been his last New Year, and who knows? It might have been the last for any of us.

The idea is simply to finish each season right and bring as much energy as possible to bear on the next.

Chapter Seven

SMALL PACKAGES

The plan certainly sounded simple enough, as basic as a duck hunter's equivalent of the pick-and-roll. The birds were too far from the waterline for a sneak, but my father, who really did enjoy seeing me shoot more than he enjoyed doing it himself, volunteered to push the flock over my head once I worked my way into position behind the dam at the far end of the pond. In theory, the result of our strategizing should have been an easy double and a good start on a teal dinner.

I managed to get behind the dam undetected, but that was the end of the predictable part of our campaign. As I waited eagerly for the birds to appear against the sky, a high-pitched whistle suddenly erupted in my ear. Then the whole flock of greenwings erupted over the top of the dam at a range measured in feet rather than yards.

I was just an inexperienced kid at the time, but to tell the truth, I'm not sure I could do much better with that shot today, forty years and a warehouse full of shells later. I finally managed to turn and snap off my first barrel at the birds going away (which is just what you're supposed to do), but I was way too flustered to hit anything but sky. There was nothing left to do but shake my head, step up on top of the dam, and signal my frustration to my endlessly patient father.

But when teal are the quarry, it pays to remember, as Yogi Berra once suggested, that it ain't over till it's over. My father began to shout and wave, and I turned to see the ducks execute a wide turn and head right back toward the little pond. I knew I still had one shell in the double, but it took me a moment to remember how to manage the selective safety. Amazingly enough, I got it right, and when the flock roared by a second time, I swung, the gun fired, and the nearest bird tumbled into the pond.

We were hunting with Bits, our wonderful all-purpose German shorthair. I've often wondered whether he was really as good in the field as I remember him, or whether those memories are subject to the kind of inflation that makes everything we did as kids seem bigger and more exciting than the cold facts might suggest. While I think he really was a great grouse and woodcock dog, our hunting venue in upstate New York didn't offer many serious tests in the water. But he didn't lose many ducks, and he wasn't about to lose this one.

And I remember the duck vividly, because it was my first teal. After all the effort required to kill it, the bird's light weight came as something of a surprise when it finally rested in my hand. But the delicacy of its markings and the brilliant green sheen of its speculum seemed nothing less than amazing. As my father congratulated me on my shot—the second, not the first—I sensed that I had fallen under a spell of sorts, and that teal were destined to play a role in my life out of all proportion to their size.

And I was right.

While there are certain important activities in which size is said not to matter, hunting generally isn't one of them. Most serious big game hunters will pass up a certain opportunity at an average animal in favor of an against-the-odds chance at an exceptional specimen. While wingshooters may not be quite as preoccupied with trophy quality, most of us acknowledge the attraction of big northern mallards, long-tailed roosters, and sage hens that look like turkeys when they flush. And how many of us would spend hours shivering in goose pits if the object of the game were measured in ounces instead of pounds? At some visceral level, the notion that bigger means better seems to arise from the same part of our DNA that makes us hunt in the first place.

The teal's popularity certainly contradicts this principle. From shovelers to mallards, puddle ducks come in a more or less continuous spectrum of size. Teal, on the other hand, are qualitatively smaller than all the rest, so much so that size alone can be used to distinguish them reliably from other ducks on the wing. A lone teal trailing a flock of mallards looks like a bug in comparison, and even hungry hunters who would be satisfied with one choice mallard on their plate can down several teal in a single sitting. But I love shooting teal, and most of the people I hunt with share that enthusiasm. Clearly, teal have found ways to transcend their diminutive size in the eye of the hunter.

Out here on the prairie where I live now, part of that appeal derives from the calendar. I love big, late-season flights of mallards as much as anyone, but opening day always evokes something special, and on the high plains the opening day of duck season means bluewings. Early teal are an evanescent phenomenon, and an unseasonable storm around the equinox can send them all south before the season opens. But on good years we can depend on bluewings to crowd the air over the decoys for a week or so right when we need them most, and the realization that every one you shoot might be the last of the year only adds to their appeal.

No duck can rival the teal's enthusiasm for decoys. Working educated mallards with a call provides it's own kind of satisfaction, but watching a flock of teal flutter guilelessly into a spread of decoys on a prairie pothole at first light remains a defining outdoor experience. Perpetually eager for company, inbound teal framed against the dawn sky virtually promise action to come. And teal have a unique way of arriving unannounced at point-blank range that can produce panic in any duck blind. Whether you first spot them descending from altitude or fluttering over the blocks, nothing justifies the effort of rising early and slogging through cold water to set out a decoy spread quite like teal.

Teal mean something special to those who enjoy the art of wingshooting. Masters of erratic flight and vertiginous turns, there is just no telling what teal will do when you finally stand up to take them. Teal have provided some of the wildest, most unpredictable shooting of my life. (They've also provided some of the most embarrassing, but that's another story.) Suffice it to say that any upland gunner who thinks he or she has it all figured out deserves to spend a morning in a blind with bluewings rocketing past at every conceivable angle. The results should prove memorable whether flavored with triumph or humiliation.

What about the dogs? I've often wondered if experienced retrievers know or care what kind of ducks they're fetching. Teal seem to arouse special enthusiasm in my Labs, but that may just reflect a canine version of the early-season excitement I feel myself when I'm shooting bluewings during the first week of October. On the other hand, dead teal look as if they belong in a retriever's mouth. While my dogs fetch geese enthusiastically enough, Labs carrying big honkers usually looks the way I feel when I'm packing an elk quarter, as if they really can't wait until they get to put the damn

thing down. Teal certainly make a more accommodating burden, and most of my dogs act as if they would be glad to tote them around all day just to show them off.

But the traits that really distinguish teal from all the rest of the puddle ducks are their unpredictability and the element of slapstick they sometimes introduce to the hunt. Years ago, my friend Ray Stalmaster and I were hunting sharptails when we crested a rise overlooking a little stock pond that contained an unexpected flock of bluewings. Ray and I both love eating teal, but the open terrain made a legitimate sneak impossible. Once again, the dam at the end of the pond offered a perfect ambush, and I suggested a flip of a coin to determine who would flush and who would shoot. "You go ahead," Ray offered gallantly. "I'll be the sacrificial lamb." I had no reason to suspect that Ray's intentions were any less sincere than my father's had been decades earlier, although subsequent events would certainly call that judgment into question.

With Sky at my side, I circled around the dam and into position. Peeking through a convenient clump of sage, I watched Ray and his Chessie march deliberately toward the far end of the pond. Just as he reached the waterline, the birds flushed and flew right at his head, allowing him an easy double.

Ray was standing with his gun broken over his arm by the time Sky and I rejoined him. As we watched his dog run down the second bird, Ray innocently asked if he could see my shotgun. I was carrying a Parker newly acquired in a complex trade, and Ray hadn't even had a chance to examine it yet. No sooner had we traded arms than the flock of teal reappeared and roared down the pond in front of us. Since I was holding Ray's unloaded gun, there wasn't much for me to do but watch as he raised my Parker and smoothly doubled again.

"Great shotgun," Ray observed as the birds hit the water.

"Great sacrificial lamb," I snorted back.

For years, visitors have wondered why Ray and I argue so loudly over who gets the honor of volunteering to flush the birds when we jump teal from stock ponds. Let the truth become a matter of record at last.

The early-morning chill feels more invigorating than uncomfortable, and the air lies so still that the coyotes yapping in
the distance sound as if they are in the blind with me. I
wouldn't mind curling up next to Sonny while we wait for
shooting light, but like all good Labs he's covered with mud
and pond water, which obligates me to enjoy his companionship at a distance. He's shivering gently, but it's a Lab's
patient duck blind shiver, the kind that reminds me of a
cat's purr. It's what retrievers do when they know they aren't
supposed to do anything but wait.

This is minimalist duck hunting: one gun, one dog, a
handful of shells, and four decoys stuck to the pond as still
and lifeless as if they have been fixed there with glue. The
blind is an old cottonwood log that has probably been lying
here on its side since the homesteading days. Fortunately,
when you're hunting early-season teal that is about all the
blind you need. While there is always a time to enjoy waterfowling's grand show, there is also a time to enjoy its simplicity.

At the first sound of wings overhead, Sonny fidgets and
gazes skyward, but it is too early to think about shooting. As
I hiss at the dog to keep him from hitting the water in a fit of
nerves, he quiets down again and we resume our wait. In
surroundings as peaceful as this, I positively enjoy waiting,
even if the dog does not.

I have mentally fixed the appointed minute on the face

of my watch, a goal toward which the long hand creeps with maddening deliberation. But one of the few things in the field you can absolutely depend on is the eventual arrival of shooting light, and the moment finally comes round at last, just as the teal do. At the sound of wings tearing through the air, I jump to my feet only to spot the birds well out of range, climbing toward the dark half of the sky. After a lifetime of duck hunting, I have just made the kind of dumb mistake that ought to embarrass a beginner.

But teal will always be teal. The birds want this pond and no other, and before I have time to wonder whether Sonny realizes what I've done, they're on a glide path right back toward the decoys. The shooting produces an odd auditory illusion: Although I never really hear the sound of the shots, the two dead birds hit the water with a splash that seems to echo all the way to the distant hills. Then it's Sonny's turn.

Black Dog Ale, my favorite local brew, sports an attractive label with a picture of a Lab and the motto No Whiners. While I agree with that sentiment in principle, I like dogs that whine while they're making water retrieves. The noise may be irritating, but it suggests a sense of uncontainable enthusiasm that strikes a nerve deep in my own heart. And despite the limited technical demands of two dead teal in a one-acre stock pond, Sonny is whining for all he's worth as he heads for shore with the first bird cupped gently in his mouth. It's just his way of letting me know there's no such thing as a boring retrieve as far as he's concerned, and I have to admit he has a point.

It's all over in half an hour. We finish the morning with two more bluewings. In aggregate, the ducks don't weigh much more than the lone sage hen we jump by accident on the hike back to the truck, but today heft seems irrelevant. You don't measure hunts like this by totaling columns of numbers. This morning's brief exercise concerns mistakes and second chances, companionship and solitude, getting more by asking for less.

This morning is about teal, and the gratitude each of us should feel whenever we have an opportunity to enjoy their presence.

Chapter Eight

DUCKS OF PARADISE

While the rugged peaks of New Zealand's Southern Alps contain some of the wildest, most spectacular scenery in the world, the rolling hills that lie along their eastern front suggest the pastoral quality one might have encountered in rural England a century ago. The countryside here suggests civilization at its tranquil best, characterized less by industry and progress than the notion that the key to a happy life stems from the ability to get along. High in the valley of the Waitaki—a beautiful glacial river whose cornflower blue waters support world-class fishing for salmon and trout—the air lay still and clear beneath a warm autumn sun. Fresh rainfall earlier in the week had left the pastures green and the local farmers smiling. This seemed to be a died-and-gone-to-heaven day by any reckoning, unless one's plans included the pursuit of waterfowl.

"No worries," our host Doug Sheldon replied when I pointed out the apparent conflict between the balmy weather and our ambitions. Since New Zealanders don't seem to worry about much of anything, his assurance didn't carry a lot of authority. However, Lori and I had already been in the country long enough to acquire our own measure of the cheerful Kiwi conviction that things will almost always work out well as long as you let them. "Let's go shoot some ducks," Doug suggested as we turned up a quiet country road that led off into the hills, and I felt myself surrender to his optimism.

And man, was I ready to shoot some ducks. I had just spent seven days trying to kill a bull tahr with my bow, an experience that left me with tough quads and an abiding respect for my quarry but no tahr. Despite a number of oh-so-close encounters, I hadn't been able to close within the intimate distance I needed for a certain shot. As much as I enjoy the challenge of the bow, after a certain amount of that kind of thing I find myself longing for the ability to reach out and swat something, an impulse best satisfied with a good double. And so as Doug stopped the car and I climbed out to open a gate separating us from a pasture containing what looked like every sheep in the world, I felt myself anticipating the sound of wings and the thump of a gun against my shoulder even more than usual.

When we all finally climbed out of the car and began to organize our gear, Jimmy and Tosh, Doug's young springers, roared around us with all the enthusiasm you'd expect from dogs that know they're going hunting. One tends to be biased by first encounters with a breed, and since none of the few springers I'd ever hunted with impressed me, I admit feeling a bit skeptical when I first saw this unlikely pair of water dogs. But we quickly made friends during the drive from Doug's farm, and my old prejudices against springers began to feel like history. And while Doug made no promises about young Tosh, he assured us Jimmy would get the job done when the time came.

Doug's plan called for us to begin by jump-shooting the pond behind a tall earthen dam in the corner of the sheep pasture. I had already explained that I preferred to shoot my ducks over decoys, but Doug promised that would come in time. Since we didn't have any decoys with us, his strategy remained a bit of a mystery, but I had already resigned myself to taking his word for things. After all, this was New Zealand, the land of no worries.

The hike across the sunny pasture felt more like the beginning of a trout fishing expedition than a duck hunt, but as we approached the base of the dam I could hear the unmistakable sound of waterfowl on the other side. After a brief discussion, Doug motioned me into position at the far corner of the dam. "Remember," he whispered as we parted. "We need to shoot a duck or two on the rise." Once we were in position, with the dogs behind Doug and Lori beside me with the camera, I checked the safety on my borrowed shotgun and nodded, and we marched forward toward the Great Perhaps.

We were hunting paradise shelducks, or parries as they are affectionately known Down Under. During the course of our tahr hunt, paradise ducks had become a familiar sight in the fields along the river bottoms. Among the largest duck species in the world, they are certainly visually impressive waterfowl. The dark drakes demonstrate brilliantly iridescent green wing specula, while the smaller but more strikingly marked hens sport solid white heads that serve as definitive field marks from hundreds of yards away. And their unique biologic origins only served to increase the fascination I felt for them. Like most of the vast Pacific's isolated island ecosystems, the New Zealand archipelago didn't enjoy a lot of natural biodiversity, at least among its fauna. From red stag to brown trout, most of New Zealand's premier sporting species are alien imports. But the parries were there from the beginning, and they remain as much a part of the area's unique native biosphere as the kiwi.

Many of the islands' indigenous species fared poorly after European colonists introduced their own favorite wildlife, but not the paradise duck. While their populations have faced intermittent declines, they are currently thriving, probably as a result of abundant food supplies in agricultural lands along fertile river bottoms. Recently, paradise duck populations have exploded throughout much of their South

Island range, and the New Zealand government has responded with liberal seasons and limits. That explains why we were hunting them in March, well in advance of the traditional May 1 waterfowl opener, which remains something of a national holiday throughout the country.

Like all experienced jump-shooters, we paced ourselves so that we crested the dam simultaneously. Because of dry conditions before the recent rain, the pond turned out to be both smaller and farther away than I expected, but paradise ducks covered its still surface like black and white confetti. A brief moment of silence followed the surprise of our appearance and then birds began to take to the air. Most of them flushed out of range, but when a lone drake rose from the waterline right beneath the dam, I dropped him. I heard another shot from Doug's direction, and then there was nothing to do but watch as the rest of the ducks disappeared into the distant sky and Jimmy completed two easy retrieves.

Ordinarily a quick jump like that would hardly have whetted my appetite, but my first good look at a paradise duck made the whole expedition worthwhile. Nearly as hefty as a snow goose, the bird's striking plumage flashed like jewelry in the afternoon sun, and he even sported a New Zealand duck tag to add to my collection. Besides, Doug had more ambitious shooting plans in mind, just as he had promised all along. While Lori and I studied and photographed the birds, he quickly whittled a pair of forked sticks from the brush along the dam face. Then he set the pair of birds on top of the dam and propped their heads up with the sticks, converting our bag into decoys.

"The rest will be back," he assured us, and then we settled in to wait.

Since Lori's waterfowling experience consisted almost exclusively of subzero midwinter hunts along our local spring creek, she found the wait very much to her liking. The afternoon felt so pleasant that I couldn't help but share her contentment despite my doubts about our ability to shoot any birds over our minimalist decoy spread on such a balmy day. Then the unmistakable nasal cry of paradise ducks in flight cut through the still air and we turned about to scan the sky in a futile attempt to locate them. Finally, a flight of six appeared right over the dam behind us, gliding toward the pond with their wings set, and I rose to take them.

Prior to our departure from Doug's farm, I had selected a 12-gauge Miroku over-under from his cabinet. While the gun shouldered and pointed naturally, it felt a bit heavy in my hands, all of which sounds like a prelude to a classic borrowed-gun excuse for poor shooting. Fortunately, it never came to that. As the birds floated by overhead, I picked a hen's white head from the middle of the flock and dropped her before I drove the barrel past the next bird in line and completed the double. Since Doug had killed a bird from his corner of the dam, little Jimmy suddenly became a busy boy.

Fortunately, all three birds lay stone dead on the pond's glassy surface, and a few minutes later our growing decoy spread started to look like the real thing.

We had barely settled back into our hiding places along the dam face when a larger flight of parries appeared over the far end of the pond, side-slipping their way downward like oversized teal. For a moment it appeared they would all land short, but half their number glided by over the dam and I dropped two more. My fascination with the ducks quickly yielded to pure enjoyment of the shooting. The shots had all been long, and each of the birds had fallen to the water with an immensely satisfying plop. Then I remembered that the handloads Doug had given me contained lead, which is perfectly legal in New Zealand. While none of us wishes to revisit supposedly dead controversies over steel shot, I'm not ashamed to admit that I hate the stuff anymore than I am ashamed to report how satisfying it felt to reach out and kill ducks dead at ambitious ranges the way we used to years ago.

And so it went for over an hour. The birds gave us just enough time between sets to congratulate each other on our good shots and forget about the rest while Jimmy earned our admiration in the pond. And hats off to the little guy; we didn't lose a single bird. By the time we finally decided to call it a day and retire to Doug's house to sample some choice selections from New Zealand's up-and-coming wine producers, we were carrying enough parries to remind me of packing big game. But one important issue remained to be settled.

During the course of our bow hunt, our local friends assured us that parries made for great shooting but poor eating. Since I love wild game on the table, that pronouncement effected me like a red flag waved in front of a bull. Besides, I've heard similar verdicts rendered about waterfowl back home often enough to regard all such opinions with healthy skepticism.

When I explained to Doug that we would really enjoy an opportunity to eat some of the ducks we had shot, he replied in typically accommodating fashion. Doug's wife, Hillary, is an accomplished chef, and after a long fishing trip up the river the following day we sat down to a splendid meal of paradise duck prepared her favorite way. While her recipe might not be my first choice for prime mallards, it certainly addressed the issue of the parries' reputed toughness and would make a fine option back home for early-season birds that deserve to be skinned. Besides, the meal proved absolutely delicious and provided a memorable farewell to a country neither Lori nor I felt the least bit like leaving.

Of all the varied activities I've enjoyed in the outdoors, none feels as distinctly American as duck hunting. Classic waterfowling demands lots of space, and as Charles Olson observes in the opening paragraph of *Call Me Ishmael*, space comes bigger here than anyplace else on earth. From water dogs to decoy carvers to the kind of conservation effort pioneered by Ducks Unlimited, the history of waterfowling might as well be rendered in red, white, and blue. While I've shot grouse, caught trout, and stalked big game with the bow from Siberia to southern Africa, the pursuit of ducks and geese has always seemed an utterly home-grown affair. It took a lazy afternoon on New Zealand's South Island to remind me that the timeless excitement of ducks and decoys travels better than most of us might imagine.

Chapter Nine

A LAKE IN THE MIDDLE OF NOWHERE

I'm going to call it Johnson Lake, the way Ann Landers's correspondents call the relatives they can't stand "Alan" or "Brittany" in order to protect a measure of anonymity. We all know who I am, of course; noms de plume have never been fashionable in outdoor writing circles. But the lake is another matter, a secret shared by a handful of friends, none of whom would ever speak to me again were I to reveal its identity to the sporting public. When you value your hunting partners as I do, the thought of that kind of ostracism sends shivers down the spine, so Johnson Lake it must be.

Dick LeBlond and I discovered the lake one summer evening nearly thirty years ago, shortly after our arrival in northeastern Montana at the beginning of a two-year volunteer stint in the Indian Health Service. We had heard rumors of its existence from several local friends, none of whom hunted ducks seriously enough to be able to provide a meaningful opinion of its waterfowling potential. But the descrip-

tions sounded intriguing, and with hunting season bearing
down on us we set out to see if we could find a source of
ducks out in the middle of the empty prairie. All the directions we received came vintage eastern-Montana style,
beginning with phrases like "Turn right five miles this side
of the old Smith place" and ending with the inevitable "You
can't miss it," a virtual guarantee to the contrary.

Undaunted, we drove for miles across the rolling terrain
north of town without finding enough water to make mud.
Just as we were about to give up, we popped over one last
rise, and there it lay: a broad fertile expanse of cattails and
standing water that seemed to stretch all the way to the horizon. Out in that dry country, the sight of so much green
grass looked nothing short of amazing. As we stood gawking,
open-mouthed at our discovery, I noticed flights of waterfowl barreling through the air at low altitude, and I knew we
had found the object of our search.

Calling it a lake involves a bit of verbal inflation, like
calling a fifteen-foot-square plywood shack on a remote
Alaska river a lodge. Except for the hidden creek bed winding somewhere through its middle, Johnson Lake scarcely
contained water deep enough to flood a pair of hip waders.
But its broad, shallow dimensions made it an ideal waterfowl
factory, and as we soon learned, its thousands of acres of
flooded grass supported every species of duck in the Central
Flyway, from teal to divers. Situated squarely in the middle

of nowhere, its shoreline never stopped suggesting the prairie's essential lonely beauty, and over the course of seasons to come I never saw another hunter there who wasn't a member of our own small circle of Johnson Lake regulars.

Unlike most standing water in eastern Montana, Johnson Lake owed nothing to dams. The lake derived from a rich prairie aquifer at the southern end of the true Saskatchewan pothole country. Although we didn't appreciate the variability of local climate conditions at the time, the early 1970s were exceptionally wet years on the western plains, and the waters of Johnson Lake stood at historically high levels. The abundance of moisture meant bountiful times for local farmers and ranchers, and they proved equally bountiful for waterfowl as well.

Our first opening day on Johnson Lake offered a splendid preview of the pleasures awaiting us there over the next two seasons. Dawn broke still and clear over the eastern sky, filling us with the peculiar despair known only to waterfowlers eager for wind to lend some life to a decoy spread and push some ducks around. But the lake still held a vast population of local bluewings, their early migration held in check by the unseasonably warm weather. Teal always seem to move according to their own fancy, and even though the mallards and pintails stayed rafted up on the larger water, flights of bluewings soon began to barrel past just over the tops of the cattails. There was a ten-bluewing limit in effect at the time, but I won't embarrass myself by admitting how many teal actually lay on the seat beside me by the time I shot my way through the first box of shells. Experienced gunners need that kind of thing from time to time, and that morning Johnson Lake provided me a lesson in humility I've never forgotten. But we did come home with enough teal for a glorious dinner, and the smell of them sizzling in the oven quickly made the sting of all those misses fade like the last dull glow of a prairie sunset.

While the lake supported a staggering population of ducks, the variety fascinated me even more than the numbers. The usual puddle ducks—mallard, teal, pintail, gadwall, and wigeon—flew in great mixed flocks, and with a point-count limit in effect, identifying species in the air before each shot provided nearly as much challenge as the shooting itself. For no particular reason, shovelers became our group's unofficial booby prize, and we took great delight in talking one another into shooting them. The open water toward the center of the marsh held good numbers of redheads and canvasbacks. On days when I found myself in a philosophical mood, I sometimes hunted them deliberately, sacrificing the bulk of my point-count limit in one calculated report from the shotgun just to be able to imagine briefly what waterfowling must have been like in the glory days on the eastern seaboard. And while there were seldom enough geese to let us pretend we were hunting them seriously, enough happened by to produce goose dinners on an incidental basis. The honkers we took by accident over duck decoys on Johnson Lake somehow felt more gratifying than many I've killed deliberately in far larger numbers.

Of course, things didn't always go quite as we planned at Johnson Lake. One August afternoon, Ray Stalmaster and I drove out to work on some blinds before we surrendered to the distractions of sharptail season. I had convinced myself that my Land Cruiser could go anywhere I could walk, and we decided to drive as close to the shoreline as possible in order to save ourselves the work of carrying all our building materials under the hot summer sun. After turning off the last gravel road, I drove out across a mile of dry mud flats before the Land Cruiser finally broke through the crust and sank to the frame. One look at our predicament convinced us we were stuck as badly as either of us could remember. We hiked several miles to the nearest farmhouse and told our sad story to its grizzled occupant. He kindly fired up his tractor and drove us back to the scene of the disaster, where he politely told us that he was looking at the dumbest bit of off-road driving he'd seen in seventy years on the prairie. We spent the rest of the afternoon rounding up enough cable to stretch from the last solid ground to the mired rig. When we finally arrived back at his farmhouse, stinking of sweat and brackish mud, he emphatically declined our offer to pay him for his trouble and invited us to stay for dinner. Those, as they say, were the good old days.

Johnson Lake offered lots of opportunities for the dogs, and their performances proved memorable on both ends of the quality spectrum. I began hunting there with a pig-headed yellow Lab named Bogey, as deserving a nominee for the title of World's Most Aggravating Retriever as any dog I've known. But I loved him the way you can only love a dog when you are young and have no children of your own, and I put up with him even when our battle of wills reached epic proportion. In retrospect, his accidental death during our first season on the lake was probably an act of mercy for all concerned. Sky was barely a year old the following year, but he already showed the courage and intelligence that helped him evolve into the best hunting Lab I've ever owned. The memory of Sky emerging from the waters of Johnson Lake as a precocious puppy, carrying his first mallard, still seems as vivid as the events of yesterday. And even after all the time I've spent in the field with dogs since then, I wonder if I've enjoyed any of it more.

Of course there were days we didn't shoot much at all, and there were days we had to work for a simple duck dinner. But the lake always had the potential to produce the grand spectacle all serious waterfowlers long for every time they gather their gear and slog through the mud toward uncertain promises of reward. One October evening, Dick and I picked up early after a long afternoon in the blind that

produced nothing but a couple of shovelers and some philosophical storytelling. As we trudged back through the cattails with the light failing around us, the year's first flight of northern mallards suddenly descended without warning, a great swirling vortex of ducks by the thousands, all apparently determined to land right on top of us. In a rare display of restraint and common sense, we unloaded our guns and let the show go on undisturbed. The noise felt deafening; feathered wings brushed against our faces in the dark. Ducks have never made me feel so small. When it was over, we listened to the warm feeding chuckles of the mallards around us in the grass and then we started back toward the truck again without exchanging a word. There just wasn't anything to say, and I'm not sure I should be trying even now.

Despite all the furious activity we sometimes enjoyed there, it was the loneliness of the place that appealed to us most in the end. We really were hunting in the middle of nowhere, without distractions, and we liked it that way. By the end of the second season, we felt as if we owned the lake, not in the sense of possession but in the sense of understanding. We didn't own anything, of course, and we had no more right to be there than anyone else. But that was part of the pleasure of Johnson Lake, and having the place mattered less than being able to appreciate what it had to offer.

But nature always represents a dynamic process, full of both giving and taking away. A decade after we left that corner of the prairie, I made friends with a hunter who had spent some time in the area during the drought years of the late 1980s. Although an avid outdoorsman who certainly should have known about a local gem like Johnson Lake, he greeted my query with a blank stare when I mentioned its name. He'd never heard of the place, and with good reason. As it turns out, once the rains stopped falling, the aquifer dried up and the lake simply disappeared. When I confirmed these facts with a few calls back to my old stomping grounds, the news effected me like a death in the family. Even though I hadn't hunted there in years, the lake still felt as if it were part of me, and I found it difficult to imagine a world without it.

But nature's capricious character works in mysterious ways. After a few seasons of generous summer rains, the lake arose once more like a phoenix. Last summer, Ray's son

Joe—who hadn't even been born back when his father and I hunted Johnson Lake together—spent his summer vacation paddling a canoe around its reborn shores, counting nesting ducks for the Montana Department of Fish, Wildlife and Parks. Just as we had done years before, he fell under the spell of the place, mosquitoes, mud, and all. And I like to think we'll all be able to get together again back there some opening day: Ray, Dick, kids, dogs, and all. That would be a fitting way to close the circle, to bring together so many essential elements of the rich lives we've enjoyed and celebrate them before the wheel of fortune turns once more.

And I'd love to show Johnson Lake to Lori. Nowadays, it's hard for me to divorce my own impressions of favorite outdoor locations from the experiences we've shared together, leaving my memories of the places I frequented years ago before I knew my wife feeling incomplete and unsettled. The shotgun has never appealed to her quite like the fly-rod or the bow, but she loves the drama of decoying birds and the excitement of the dog work and the way prairie sunrises reach out and beg for attention from the camera lens. Perhaps she just needs a place like Johnson Lake to make the whole equal the sum of all those various parts. I'd love to have an opportunity to find out.

The public's appreciation of the outdoors tends to glorify stereotypes. Out where I live, the conventionally scenic western part of Montana invariably draws the tourist's eye, while the prairies to the east arouse the impulse to put the foot on the accelerator and get the prairie over with as quickly as possible. To each his own, I suppose. In this chapter, I've tried to offer personal testimony to the contrary. And if I've done my job, the reader will understand why solitude matters, where memory reigns, and how a lake in the middle of nowhere can wind up feeling like the center of the universe after all.

Chapter Ten

IMPOSSIBLE LITTLE BIRDS

M y friend Arthur Seeligson and his family have been around Texas forever. Arthur's great-grandfather served as Galveston's second mayor. A faded photograph hangs in the kitchen of the Seeligson hacienda, showing a distant relative with an arm draped fraternally about the shoulder of none other than Pancho Villa. "A cold-blooded killer," Arthur observed with a nod. "But an interesting one."

Lori and I had traveled south to Arthur's ranch to hunt quail, and we'd spent our first afternoon together chasing bobwhites behind a brace of hard-working pointers in traditional and enjoyable fashion. Over breakfast on the second morning of our visit, Arthur rather improbably suggested a snipe hunt. Given south Texas's arid terrain, it occurred to me that this proposal might be the beginning of some kind of joke, complete with nets, bells, and whistles. But while I appreciate Arthur's sense of humor, he doesn't kid around much when it comes to hunting. And since we happened to know how much he loves to eat snipe, we set off anticipating a real snipe hunt rather than the preadolescent version of foolish goings-on in the midnight woods.

Accustomed to hunting snipe in cool, wet places, I soon found myself forced to abandon everything my prior experience had taught me about the species. Most of my previous encounters with snipe had come pretty much by accident while engaged in the pursuit of other birds, from teal to creek-bottom pheasants. Back when I lived in Alaska, we sometimes found snipe concentrated on the tide flats in deliberately huntable numbers, in which case shooting them consisted of swapping duck loads for No. 8s and walking through the grass until we jump-shot a snipe dinner or ran out of shells. But none of those earlier encounters prepared me for what was about to follow on that balmy December morning in south Texas.

After a short drive from the ranch house, Arthur led us to a low spot in a field that consisted of little more than a dozen acres of mud. As we eased into position, snipe began to rise like smoke, filling the air with their harsh cries as they swirled away into the sky. We all held our fire, partly because most of the snipe flushed out of range, but also because they rose accompanied by an avian menagerie of shorebirds, and none of us wanted to make an embarrassing mistake. As the air finally grew still once more, Arthur grinned in anticipation and reassured us that the snipe hunt had not yet begun.

And indeed it hadn't. After a ten-minute wait (during which I admit feeling ever so slightly foolish), snipe began to filter back toward the little pan in singles and pairs, diving down out of the sky like aircraft piloted by suicidal drunks. Our friend Dick Negley finally broke the silence as he rose and dropped a single that tumbled into the middle of the pond where Beau, his amiable golden, quickly scooped it up on the run. "Snipe!" Lori suddenly cried from behind me.

"No it's not," I replied as I followed the line of her outstretched arm.

"Yes it is!" she argued back.

By that time I could appreciate the long bill protruding from the leading edge of the bird's profile, at which point I shouldered the gun, tracked the inbound bundle of feathers through a glorious series of curlicues, and missed. Twice.

So began a long but fascinating hour. I realize that when I write about the outdoor life the recollection of my own shooting sometimes sounds mildly inflated. In fact, these descriptions are neither calculated nor untrue. It's not that I'm a great shot in any technical sense of the term. I just hunt a lot, and as a consequence I generally hit what I shoot at. But turnabout is fair play, and in this spirit of candor I offer the following frank admission: I missed a hell of a lot of snipe that morning.

I won't bore anyone with borrowed-gun excuses. The fact is that pass-shooting snipe can be a very tricky proposition. Most game birds fly with the general intention of getting from point A to point B in reasonably expedient fashion. Not so snipe, who seem to regard the process of flight the same way a teenager might regard test driving a sports car. Furthermore, between the yellowlegs and the mourning doves (not in season at the time, unfortunately), there were lots of distractions in the air, and raising one's head from the stock to reconfirm the identity of a target almost certainly guarantees a miss. I found that the best way to address this problem was to identify one bird a long way out and track it visually all the way into range, ignoring everything else overhead. Then when I missed, at least I knew exactly what I was missing.

It wasn't that it couldn't be done, as Dick proved quite ably with one of his customary displays of fine shooting. And after squandering my first handful of shells, I even managed to kill a few birds myself. But each time one of those little long-billed shuttlecocks fell out of the sky I felt vaguely amazed, and I never did reach the point of expecting to drop a bird with every shot. The challenge made me concentrate on the shooting as I had not done in some time, and in the end I appreciated the misses as much as the birds we collected and hauled back to the kitchen in ever so slightly subdued triumph.

The following morning we rose to a breakfast of huevos rancheros, quail, and snipe. And on that distinct culinary note, Lori and I finally prepared to return home, where another high-plains winter already lay in wait. We all promised to meet back at our home in Montana the following autumn, where our friendship had begun years earlier, through one of those strange series of coincidences that sometimes bring outdoor enthusiasts together in unlikely fashion. We had come for the quail and had enjoyed their pursuit, but I already knew that I would remember the unique shooting at the mud hole long after the memory of the bobwhite and the pointers had faded.

Snipe: the impossible little birds.

On the afternoon before the opening day of duck season, the grass on the tide flats still stood tall before the first hard frost, but a dusting of fresh snow on the peaks to the west reminded me of the season's shifting momentum. I had noticed a nice smattering of puddle ducks on the potholes during the flight down from the cabin, but the waterfowl remained little more than a matter of passing interest. Silver salmon held my attention that afternoon; the ducks could wait until the following day.

I took the long way to the fishing hole, working my way upstream along the river so I could scout the water. The tracks in the mud along the bank confirmed that several other fishermen had beat me to the pool earlier that morning, but they had all walked on four legs rather than two. A series of strong boils where the clear-water tributary met the glacial river confirmed that salmon still lay right where I'd imagined them. After rigging my rod and tying on a streamer, I worked a loop of line into the air and let it drop. Three strips later, the rod tip went down hard and the fish took to the air like a promise fulfilled.

Since this is a hunting story, I'll spare readers a detailed description of the next hour's events. Suffice it to say that by the time I broke my rod down and headed back to the airplane, I had caught enough silvers to satisfy my interest in fish for days to come. I kept one to cook for my friends back at the cabin that night, and one was enough. With that mission pleasantly accomplished, I decided to take a shortcut back across the tide flat to the airplane. Thirty yards into the grass, the rough sound of wings erupted underfoot. I was on edge anyway because of the bears, and the sudden explosion of noise practically turned me inside out. But it was only a snipe, and as I tracked its erratic flight with an imaginary double I felt myself yielding to the intangible mental transition between summer and hunting season.

The first few birds didn't really arouse my interest, but by the time I had kicked a dozen birds out of a hundred-yard stretch of grass, I realized that I had blundered into the middle of an unusual bounty. The birds seemed to be daring me to shoot them as they zigzagged away at the goofiest angles imaginable. Plenty of snipe rose in front of me during the hike back to the airplane, and I hesitated to think how many more I might have flushed with a dog. I did not know where the birds had come from or how long they planned to remain, but by the time I landed back at the cabin, I had come to a decision. That year, my opening day of duck season would include an afternoon snipe hunt.

The following morning, dawn broke clear and still over my makeshift duck blind, and for the next two hours the pace of the shooting felt as relaxed as the weather. As I shot a handful of birds in unhurried fashion, I reminded myself that opening days are a matter of tradition rather than body count. Sky had reached the point in his career when he hunted because he liked to and not because he had anything to prove, and his workmanlike attitude suited the mood perfectly. He didn't do anything brilliant, but I never had to ask him to. As I picked up the decoys and started back to the cabin, we left the field with the satisfaction of knowing that every duck I shot at was resting in the back of the game vest. Granted that wasn't a lot of birds, but the day felt so pleasant that neither of us really cared.

Over breakfast, my friends and I chatted easily about shooting and the dog work until there wasn't anything more that needed to be said. Once we'd cleaned up the dishes and put them away, I dug an old box of trap loads from the chaos beneath my bunk and announced that I was going snipe hunting. I invited everyone to come along, but the idea evidently sounded preposterous. As the others dispersed to pluck ducks and tinker with gear, I found myself walking down to the little grass strip alone, except for the dog.

Sky had logged his share of time in the air over the years, and as we took off for the river he sat alertly in the back seat as if he might be called upon to navigate. The flight was so short that our trajectory resembled a baseball's more than an airplane's, and it was sobering to realize that it would probably have taken me days to cover the same ground on foot. But that's Alaska, where the going always proves easier with a bit of air beneath your wings.

This time when I landed in the dirt beside the river, I pulled the shotgun rather than the fly-rod out of the airplane, and as I remembered the bear tracks in the mud the previous day, its heft felt especially welcome in my hands. In fact, I knew full well that the shotgun wouldn't be a whole lot more help than the fly-rod if it came to that, and as I stuffed my pockets with shells, I sat Sky down for some last minute council. "Remember, buddy!" I barked into his face with all the authority I could muster. "No bears!" He responded with one of his *Oh, please!* looks and then I dropped a pair of shells into the gun and we set off into the grass.

We hadn't covered fifty yards before he nosed the first snipe into the air. Even though I was anticipating the rise, the bird's raspy bronk and the buzz of its wings caught me off guard, and I snapped the stock to my shoulder awkwardly. The shooting over the decoys that morning had been kid stuff, but the snipe's erratic flight proved another matter and I missed cleanly. Chiding myself for my incompetence, I reloaded just in time to hear another bird flush behind me, and I turned and dropped it in a glorious little puff of feathers. Then it was time for Sky to do what retrievers are supposed to do best, and he did.

Despite their noisy flight and the surprise they generate when they flush, snipe turn out to be remarkably tiny birds. When Sky finally emerged from the grass, bearing his prize, there wasn't much to see except an elongated bill dangling from the corner of his mouth like a toothpick. But I accepted his offering gratefully and scratched his head before rechecking the safety and turning back toward the cover, for it seemed important to reassure him that despite their size these birds were what we were after. An unnecessary precaution as it turns out; the definition of a bird dog remains the ability to distinguish game birds from all the rest, and Sky had been at this way too long to miss any opportunity for a retrieve.

Craziness ruled for nearly an hour, with snipe skittering away across the beautiful, barren flats at one wild angle after another. I finally managed to pocket the bird I needed to complete a limit just before I exhausted my supply of shells. As we completed the long circle back through the grass to the airplane, the salt mud sucked eagerly at my boots and a determined cloud of bugs whined hungrily about my face. The fatigue of the long day had finally caught up with me. A wayward teal rocketed by overhead, but I didn't even bother to raise my gun. Sometimes in the outdoors, knowing when to quit can be as important as knowing when to pull the trigger, and the snipe had brought me to just that point of closure.

My vest full of snipe aroused plenty of interest back in the cabin that night, and after another relaxed round of waterfowl over decoys the following morning I led my friends on an expedition back to the snipe fields. This time we really looked as if we meant business: two Super Cubs, three guns, three dogs, and every light load we could scrounge from the neglected corners of the cabin. As we set off across the flats I found myself remembering early Winslow Homer sporting studies and the grand old traditions of American marsh hunting. Smug and impressed by my own capacity for discovery, I couldn't wait to share the novel pleasures of another snipe hunt with my company.

The weather on the second day of duck season felt even balmier than it had on the first. Warm air lay quietly above the flats, and swarms of insects rose to greet us. Sweat began to build as I labored through the mud. No matter; after my experience the day before, I felt certain that we would all soon be too busy shooting snipe to notice. Sky led the charge through the cover, and I settled into the determined pace of the hunt as I waited for the first noisy flush to rise from the mud beneath our feet.

But this time it was not to be. Sensing some gathering of the seasons that escaped us, the birds had all departed overnight. It took two long hours to prove the point, but finally there was nothing to do but acknowledge that the birds had snookered us in the end, proving all over again just how hard it can be to get the last laugh on nature. "Great snipe hunt," someone observed as we staggered back to the airplanes without having fired a shot, and then we broke our guns and loaded the dogs and set off back to the cabin to devote ourselves to more conventional duck season pursuits.

As we lifted off above the alders, I banked the Cub around for one last pass over the flats, as if I needed to confirm that the scene of this humiliation was really the same place the snipe had led us on such a glorious chase the day before. That's when I saw the bear. Standing still as a statue in a patch of brush between the flats and the river, he seemed to be waiting for the clamor to recede so he could get on with his business, whatever that might be. While his size and the shaggy translucence of his auburn coat made him look obvious from the air, he seemed to feel well hidden in the brush, and I wondered how many times I had walked right by him during the course of the last three days. Then he slid by underneath the wing and disappeared, and the lonely expanse of grass and brush looked as empty as I remembered it from ground level all over again.

Great snipe hunt! I thought to myself above the throb of the engine, echoing the disappointment expressed earlier by my hunting partners. *Impossible little birds!* Snipe hunts are supposed to be a joke, after all, and true to form, this time the joke had been on us. But while I didn't doubt that I would be hearing about this one for months to come, I still remembered the racket the birds made as they flushed and the satisfaction I felt every time I dropped one into the grass. It had been a great snipe hunt, even if no one knew it but Sky and me, and in the end those seemed to be the only opinions that truly mattered.

Chapter Eleven

FIRST GEESE

Memory distorts and confuses in a manner analogous to what Von Clausewitz termed the fog of war. Over a decade has passed since we set off together into the marsh, and after all these years I only remember two things clearly. Both pertain to size: the delicacy of my daughter's hand in mine as we walked through the darkness toward the water, and the bulk of the geese dragging from the strap across my shoulder when we returned.

The harsh sound of an alarm clock can evoke wildly divergent responses, depending on when one hears it. During the workweek, the racket usually conveys bad news, interrupting dreams and signaling an enforced return to the world of obligations and responsibilities. But on weekends during duck season, the cry of an alarm in a darkened bedroom sounds more like an invitation. When the clock sounded that morning I leapt out of bed as brainlessly eager as a retriever on the trail of a running pheasant, dressing in the dark half asleep and aware of nothing until the first welcome smell of the coffee rose to fill the kitchen.

My daughter Genevieve was seven years old that season, an assertive kid in all respects: a daredevil on the ski slopes, an age-group soccer-field terror, fearless on the back of her horse. No stranger to the outdoors, she had accompanied me on various adventures in the field since her early childhood in Alaska, where she was born. But somehow she had missed the grand spectacle of a real goose hunt: the anxiety of the birds' long, cautious approach, the adrenaline rush of the shooting, and the choreography of the dog work that follows. The invitation I offered the night before came flavored with uncertainty on my own part, for I couldn't expect any seven-year-old to rise in the dark, slog through the mud, and shiver in anticipation of an event that might not even take place. I should have known better.

As I turned away from the coffeepot to walk downstairs and wake her up, she suddenly appeared before me on her own, alive with more youthful enthusiasm than any adult should be asked to endure at that hour of the morning. She stood already dressed in the clothing we had laid out the night before, complete from camo cap to rubber boots. I offered her cereal but—suddenly a big girl—she wanted a cup of coffee. Remembering the subtle conspiracies that evolved between my father and me when my mother wasn't around to object, I complied, cutting hers with powdered cocoa, cautioning her not to burn her lips and offering my sympathy when she did so anyway.

Dick and Ray arrived shortly thereafter. We had been studying the geese for a week, tracking them backward from the fields with our binoculars through a series of prairie potholes until we finally located the one they called home. Real goose hunters may disdain shooting birds on their home water, but I dislike setting up in stubble fields as much as I enjoy watching dawn break over marshes with their attendant population of ducks, shorebirds, and incidental wildlife. Spooking the geese from their favorite pond seemed a small price to pay for hunting them under our own terms. This would likely be our one and only chance at these birds, but we all agreed to accept the consequences of our decision.

I knew I was imposing heavily on my hunting partners when I asked to include Jenny in our plans. Important shoots aren't necessarily compatible with youthful concepts of goose blind discipline, and we had invested a lot of effort into setting up this hunt. But Dick and Ray appreciated the value of involving kids in outdoor plans even if doing so might cost some shooting, and they both regarded Jenny as one of their own. They had already let me know that any hesitation I might have felt on their behalf about bringing Jenny along was wasted on them. That's the kind of selflessness that defines valued hunting partners, and I appreciated it.

The marsh we planned to hunt lay over an hour's drive north of town, but the miles passed quickly, eased along by a steady stream of reminiscence about the time Dick, Ray, and I had spent together in the remote northeastern corner of Montana years before. Hunting stories are like vintage wines: some deserve to be done away with at the earliest opportunity, while others only improve with the passage of time, gaining in texture and complexity. These were among the best, full of ducks and birds and dogs no longer with us. Jenny listened wide-eyed and eager as if she were hearing the stuff of tribal legend, and perhaps she was.

The geese had already risen in the dark and departed for the fields by the time we arrived at the marsh. The October sky lay still and clear overhead as light began to swell across the eastern plains. A shower the previous day had turned the track across the stubble field to gumbo and left the air full of the pungent aroma of sage. Laboring under the burden of the decoys, we slipped and slid our way down to the waterline and set to work. Jenny proved eager to help, and at first I assigned her the task of mounting the heads on the shells, a mission she could accomplish perfectly well on dry land. But setting the decoys in position along the edge of the water proved too much temptation for her to resist, and before I could stop her she was out in the mud and over her boots. I really couldn't bring myself to scold her, since I remembered doing exactly the same thing when I was her age, no matter how hard my own father tried to discourage me.

Marshes offer more natural blind opportunities than stubble fields, which is one reason I prefer to hunt geese over water. Field blinds are almost always a nuisance to build and uncomfortable to occupy, and even after all the effort of their construction they usually leave me feeling conspicuous as a squashed bug on a freshly cleaned windshield. But an inviting perimeter of dense cattails surrounded the marsh that morning, and once the decoys lay in place, all we had to do was set up four folding stools in the middle of the reeds. We had not yet experienced the season's first hard frost, and the cattails stood so thick we could barely see each other five yards apart. Waterfowling doesn't offer a lot of free lunches, but as we settled comfortably into position I felt as if we were enjoying one of the rare ones.

The high-pitched sound of wings overhead greeted the arrival of shooting light, and soon thereafter we noticed a flock of ducks fluttering across the water in our direction. Disciplined goose hunters might have let them pass, but when they set their wings above the decoys we all yielded at once to the urge to rise and take them. Jenny shouted with excitement at the sound of the shooting and the sight of the fallen birds kicking on the water, and when the dogs leapt eagerly into action I knew we had made the right decision. After all, a bird in the hand...

I had brought Sherry along that morning, a young female yellow Lab of unproven potential that badly needed an opportunity to work without distraction from Skykomish. Ray was hunting with Lester, a dark, hulking Chessie with the most heart-stopping water entry of any dog I've ever seen. Side by side, the two looked like Beauty and the Beast. As they set off to collect the handful of downed ducks, Sherry picked her way delicately through the mud like a cover girl worried about her makeup, while Lester crashed through the shallows like a water buffalo in heat. But each in their own way, they accomplished their mission, and Jenny giggled in delight as if we had staged the show for her exclusive benefit.

With the welcome distraction of the ducks behind us, we settled back to wait, a process with which all goose hunters must inevitably come to terms. Doing nothing can be one of childhood's most daunting assignments, but Jenny handled the responsibility cheerfully. We passed the time by plucking the ducks and practicing with the goose call, a distraction that at least relieved her of any obligation to silence. After an hour of empty skies, she plainly felt delighted by her progress, and it was all I could do to get her to stop calling long enough to let me listen for the real thing.

When we finally heard the first quavering chorus of geese in the distance, the birds were still too far off to see. But as we brought the dogs to order and studied the southern horizon, an undulating line of dots appeared against the sky at last. I knew at once by their attitude in flight that they were headed toward us, and only some silly mistake on our part could keep us from killing our share. I liked the look of the decoy spread and felt confident about our hiding place in the cattails. Unless we somehow lost our heads on the birds' final approach or shot like amateurs, Jenny was minutes away from watching her first geese tumble from the sky.

When several shooters share a goose blind, silly errors commonly derive from excess courtesy and failure to communicate. In the company of sportsmen, everyone wants to avoid standing prematurely and shooting birds out from under other members of the party, but too much deference only results in birds passing in and out of range without anybody shooting. Recognizing that even poor choices can be superior to no choice at all, we have developed two simple rules to avoid that kind of mishap: We always elect a leader, and the leader's decisions are always immune to debate (at least until after the fact). That morning, Ray served as jaegermeister by popular acclaim, and as the birds began their slow, deliberate descent toward our position, I concentrated on doing nothing until he declared it time.

As the sky overhead filled with the deafening sound of geese, the urge to stare upward and track their progress felt all but unbearable. I knew better, of course: Years of experience had taught me how quickly a face's pale flash can ruin a perfect exercise in deceit. But I still remembered sitting in painful silence beside my own father in duck blinds years earlier, and how desperately I longed to ignore his whispered admonition to *Look down!* All I could do was offer the same instruction to Jenny and hope she understood its importance, and she did. Then Ray suddenly cried *Take them!* and we all rose together.

Whenever three guns face a hundred birds, simple statistics would suggest the improbability of two shooters locking onto the same target at once. Experienced hands know better. One or two low fliers always seem to demand the eye's attention, and it's amazing how often I've watched one of those birds fall to a hunting partner's shot just as I was about to slap my own trigger. After all the effort we had invested in this hunt, I didn't feel like walking away with two birds shot three times apiece, so I made myself ignore the handful of honkers hanging directly over the decoys and turned to concentrate on my own sector. A goose shuddered and collapsed at the sound of my first barrel. As the rest of the flock scattered skyward, I drove the gun through the outline of a second bird flaring overhead and crumpled it. From the corner of my eye, I watched Ray track one last goose and roll it midair with the third shot from his ancient pump, and then the marsh stood oddly silent once again.

The release of tension felt all but palpable. While Jenny giggled in a burst of inarticulate excitement, we three adults scarcely acted more restrained. Fair enough; geese make kids of all of us, and that's the point of hunting them. While Sherry and Lester went to work, we emerged from our hiding place in the cattails and approached the waterline to watch their performance, for we all found the dog work as much a part of the show as the shooting.

Six birds lay stone dead upon the surface of the water, and Lester and Sherry made short work of them. No one admitted to a miss, and as we counted shots, Ray and I each remembered his first goose setting its wings and sailing toward the brush that lined the marsh's outflow. We hacked the dogs in to our sides and sent them, and five minutes later Lester emerged with the last goose cradled in his mouth, proving that none of us had lied about the accuracy of our shooting.

Lester had barely completed the retrieve when Jenny's young ears—uncompromised by too many years of shotguns—detected the sound of another flock of geese in the distance. We hurried back into the cattails just in time to receive the second set of the morning. Jenny did the calling. With our goose dinner a matter of record, we felt free to savor the measured pace of their approach before Dick and I stood up and dropped the two birds we needed to complete our limit. Then it was time to stand and stretch in the morning sun before we began the long task of picking up the decoys. When we finally headed back to the truck, the weight of the game strap over my shoulder evoked the memory of packing big game from the field and provided the final impression of the morning.

Over a decade has passed since that brief interlude on the prairie. Dick has moved east to Iowa, but we stay in touch as well as distances allow. Lester and Sherry are dead, replaced by dogs that demonstrate their own unique catalog of strengths and weaknesses in the field. Ray still lives just up the hill, and we hunt together as often as we can, even though those early alarm clocks sometimes sound a little less inviting than they did a few years back. Jenny is busy preparing for college. We've endured our share of adolescent ups and downs, but we'll get through it. I know we will.

The true texture of childhood can only be appreciated in retrospect. It isn't that youth is really wasted on the young; so much of it simply goes over their heads. In the end, each of us is left with nothing but a patchwork of memories, collections of bits and pieces that somehow manage to fit together like an old-fashioned quilt: a father's lessons in goose blind discipline, dogs that offer amazing performances in the water, small hands and large hands together in the dark.

And first geese, the kind that can never be taken away.

Chapter Twelve

INCIDENTAL PLEASURES

The weather that morning left me surrounded by oddly conflicting impressions. The little pothole's surface lay still as crystal, leaving the decoys set against a reflective, crimson background as the sun crept over the horizon far across the sage to the east. Only a cynic or a fool could deny the aesthetic pleasures of a sunrise like that. On the other hand, serious waterfowlers rarely welcome calm mornings, despite their obvious charm. Experience soon teaches that moving birds are a phenomenon of foul weather, proving all over again that beauty really does lie in the eye of the beholder. Visits to duck blinds usually involve compromises between serenity and comfort on one hand and lots of shooting on the other, and real duck hunters always stand out by virtue of their preference for the latter. Despite the daybreak's breathtaking beauty, I would have traded all that technicolor for a cold front's dull grays in a heartbeat.

In fact, the complete duck hunter must learn to become both a predator and a philosopher, two character traits that at first glance seem difficult to reconcile. But as a student of natural history, I recognized years ago that we learn most about the world we inhabit when we intrude upon it as little as possible. Werner Heisenberg won the 1932 Nobel Prize in physics for elucidating that principle with regard to subatomic particles, and when my own observation of game birds and animals taught me the same lesson, I felt delighted to find myself in such illustrious company.

This hunt took place early one October, well before most of Montana's migratory avian species had started to gather prior to their annual fall departure. My goal that morning was nothing more ambitious than a teal dinner, and the only urgency I felt derived from the realization that the opportunity to fulfill it would disappear right along with the bluewings on the heels of the season's first hard cold snap. Thanks to the balmy weather, it came as no surprise when the first flock of birds to swoop down to the water that morning weren't waterfowl at all, but western meadowlarks. While I hadn't set off that morning as a bird watcher, the feel of the day made it easy to settle back and accept what the prairie chose to offer.

About that time, the Montana legislature was busy debating a motion to replace the meadowlark as the state bird. According to its critics (who wanted to replace it with the magpie, of all things), the meadowlark was nothing but

a loud, gaudy showoff that offended the state's full-time residents by abandoning Big Sky country at the first hint of
winter. Talks the talk but can't walk the walk, the complaint
against the meadowlark went. Other than some quiet pride
in the realization that I lived in a state willing to argue such
matters at public expense, I hadn't given the issue a lot of
thought. But all of a sudden I had dozens of the newly con-
troversial birds splashing around in front of my blind like
kids at a swimming hole during summer vacation.

And I must admit that I never realized before that morning how fastidious meadowlarks can be when it comes time
for their daily bath. With the males' golden chests bared
against the morning sun, they preened and fluttered through
the water inches in front of my blind, always stopping just
short of total immersion. I had taken these birds for granted
on countless gates and fence posts over the years, but now I
felt as if I were truly seeing them for the first time. And it
wasn't just their numbers or the magical quality of the
morning light upon their plumage that made the experience
unprecedented. It was our sudden proximity under innocent
circumstances, an intimate relationship made possible only
by the hunter's knack for patience and camouflage. By the
time the dog finally snuffled and spooked the flock, I had
nearly forgotten about the duck hunt.

I had barely recovered from the meadowlarks when a
compelling sound of wing-beats rose somewhere off in the

distance. I reflexively reached for the shotgun, but by the time my hand closed upon the stock I realized that the latest arrivals weren't waterfowl either. Nonetheless, something about the sound had gone straight to the part of the brain that says *take 'em*, ducks or otherwise. Finally I recognized the familiar chuckling call of sharptails and settled back to enjoy the second unscheduled act of the morning.

Just like African sand grouse, the flock landed a stone's throw from the shore and proceeded toward the waterline on foot. I have no idea how many sharptails I've killed on the wing, but I usually encountered them as noisy gray blurs against the sky or, occasionally, during the late season, as wary sentries perched high in the barren branches of some windswept tree. Once again, circumstances had treated me to an utterly unexpected perspective on what I regarded as a familiar species. The grouse looked oddly soft and rotund as they waddled down to the water, and it was all I could do to keep the dog quiet enough to let them finish their stately approach. Suddenly, there were decisions to face.

I've spent my share of time as an observer of natural history and I've learned a lot in the process. But just as there is a time to observe, so there is a time to engage. Early-season sharptails happen to be one of my favorite upland game birds on the table, and as the vanguard finally drew within shotgun range I realized that my stint as a bird-watcher had reached its limits. To the dog's obvious delight, I rose with the double cradled in my hands, and when the birds flushed I dropped a pair of them going away. I'm sure some wing-shooting purist might find fault with this unorthodox grouse ambush, but its conclusion left me perfectly satisfied.

As I recall, a flock of teal eventually dropped in to visit, and I shot one or two. Memory has blurred the details of the expected events. I do know that we dined on grouse that night, with no regrets. But what I remember best from the hours I spent in the blind that quiet morning is the play of the sunlight across the meadowlarks' breasts and the absolute surprise of the sharptails' unexpected appearance. Those who hunt in order to keep score will protest that meadowlarks and sharptails have nothing to do with waterfowling.

I beg to differ.

One dull gray afternoon years ago I sat hunkered in a swath of cattails beside another remote lick of prairie water, awaiting the arrival of what I hoped would be the year's first flight of migrating northern mallards. A dozen old plastic decoys bobbed gently in front of my makeshift blind. It wasn't much of a spread, but the ducks were either going to show up or they weren't, and I knew full well the degree of effort I chose to invest in the invitation would have little to do with the outcome of the hunt.

Waiting for waterfowl sometimes resembles waiting for Godot, but I had chosen to ignore the day's existential implications by nodding off to sleep. Suddenly a loud report shattered the air and I looked up just in time to see a marsh hawk straining upwards into the sky. One of the blocks faltered briefly on the surface like a miniature Titanic before it listed to one side and sank gracefully beneath the surface, its hull punctured by a set of steely talons. Obviously, the decoy had fooled something unintended.

The remarkable element of that close encounter was its absolute novelty. After all the hours I'd logged in duck blinds, that was the first time I'd ever seen a raptor strike a decoy. Intuitively, one would think that setting out countless imitations of hawk chow before countless numbers of hawks would produce some hits, but that hardly ever proves to be the case. In fact, I've watched innumerable marsh hawks glide past duck decoys without so much as a second look. Do hawks kill ducks less frequently than we imagine? Does their superior vision consistently allow them to avoid wasting time and energy on catalog imitations? Such questions must remain part of the mystery of the waterfowler's world.

Of course, raptors aren't the only predators to enjoy the bounty of good duck habitat. Over the years, I've enjoyed close encounters with killers ranging from grizzlies to rattlesnakes while duck hunting, including a varied assortment of foxes, coyotes, raccoons, skunks, and bobcats. The juxtaposition of predators and waterfowl hardly seems surprising. Wetlands serve as a magnet for wildlife of all kinds, and duck hunters come in four-legged models as well as two. It's finally up to each of us to decide whether to regard our fellow inhabitants of the food chain's upper stories as company or competition.

Therein lies a legitimate difference of opinion among those charged with managing North America's waterfowl habitat. Deliberately reducing predator numbers near critical wetlands seems an obvious way to enhance waterfowl production, as some knowledgeable and responsible parties have suggested. In fact, the complex relationship between populations of predators and prey forms the basis for some of wildlife biology's most enduring arguments. Suffice it to say that there are no easy answers.

Personally, I've chosen to bypass the question of whether or not eliminating predators will increase duck numbers. My instincts tell me that when habitat thrives, waterfowl will thrive right along with it. Build a field and they will come. More to the point, I enjoy seeing raccoon tracks etched in frozen mud and listening to coyotes yap while I'm setting out decoys at dawn. In fact, I regard such incidental pleasures as an essential part of the waterfowling experience, and working a little harder for my ducks over the course of the season seems a small price to pay for the enjoyment they provide. Of course, not everyone will agree with this brief editorial opinion, but that's why we live in a free country. Constructive argument will always benefit conservation, as long as it doesn't compromise the four things wildlife needs to survive: clean air, clean water, adequate food, and a place to live.

Back when I was a toddler, my mother used to wear a muskrat coat during the cold winter months in northern New York. While I can still vividly recall the luxurious feel of that rich fur against my cheeks, I find it difficult to associate that memory with the sight of a swimming muskrat. In the water, muskrats move with their own kind of grace, but they still look like, well...rats. As the gradually widening V crossed the surface of the pond toward the blind, I found myself imaging the animal's curved yellow incisors and naked scaly tail, an image plainly difficult to reconcile with the warmth, nurture, and comfort my mother's coat evoked during my early childhood.

But then the muskrat reached the waterline in front of the blind and climbed out on the bank to enjoy the cattails he'd carried across the pond like exaggerated green whiskers. The warm sun effected an immediate transformation as the animal's coat began to dry. Pond water beaded up on the guard hairs, forming individual droplets that began to sparkle like jewels, while the rich auburn undercoat gathered the early-morning light. *Abracadabra*...as if by magic, my visitor wasn't a rat anymore and I found myself remembering my mother's fur coat all over again.

Duck blinds seem to specialize in just such quiet epiphanies, and learning to appreciate them certainly helps time

pass whenever waterfowl decline to honor hunters with their presence. But a steady diet of natural philosophy can grow just as tedious as thoughtless shooting. That's why I won't even pretend I resented the interruption the first ducks caused that morning. A half dozen gadwalls strong, the little flock caught me totally by surprise as they slipped into the decoys unannounced. Transformed from observer to participant once again, I quickly confirmed the birds' identity, rose, and fired both barrels. To the dog's obvious delight, two birds hit the water stone dead. While Sky surged forward toward the first, I fumbled with fresh shells in case the remainder of the flock did something foolish, but they didn't. Finally, there was nothing left to do but dodge the inevitable fountain of dog spray, scratch some ears, and settle into doing nothing all over again.

It's really remarkable what a small percentage of the duck hunter's time actually involves killing ducks. Every brief flurry of shooting represents countless hours invested in a catholic array of ancillary activities: scouting, building blinds, training dogs, loading shells, fiddling with calls and decoys...and above all, just plain waiting. At least in its classic form—from a blind, over decoys—waterfowling demands a staggering amount of time spent not doing much. All of which explains why true pleasure in the field has less to do with bag limits and fast shooting than the ability to wait with grace...and to appreciate the incidental pleasures of a world few but the waterfowler will ever see so clearly.

Chapter Thirteen

THE GREAT DUCK-OFF

Don't call me Ishmael.

In fact, I love the sea, and after many years on the plains of Montana, I missed it so badly that we bought a second home in southeast Alaska just so we could watch the tide roll in and out while we enjoyed its bounty on our table. I love the smell of salt air and the abundance of wildlife that proximity to the ocean provides. But the version of the sea with which I'm most familiar—the North Pacific—has always engendered a sense of respect barely removed from terror, not without basis in fact. Back when I flew bush planes in Alaska, I felt at home in the air even under circumstances that made my passengers shiver. Out at sea, on the other hand, I never forgot that nothing but a few thin inches of wood or fiberglass separated me from instant disaster. As much as I loved being there, I never let the ocean allow me to relax.

My old friend Bob May has spent as much time plying treacherous waters as anyone I know. Bob has lived on the north shore of Kodiak Island for years, and his chosen job description—registered guide and commercial fisherman—has left him with a deeply intuitive knowledge of the sea and its hazards. If I were going to send Lori and the kids across Shelikoff Straight in a small boat, Bob would be the one I'd want at the helm. But even after all those years in Kodiak waters, Bob and I share one interesting characteristic. Once he leaves shore, Bob never relaxes either.

We left the beach on Whale Island under clear azure skies. A brief storm had swept through overnight, and Kodiak's mainland peaks lay beneath a pristine blanket of snow. Whale Pass looked like a polished mirror beneath the calm autumn skies, and as we pulled away from shore, we watched a flight of puffins skim past us with their brilliant facial marking plainly reflected from its surface. The run inland toward the bay we planned to hunt had all the makings of a milk run. The trouble is, on Kodiak there's no such thing.

As we headed off to the southeast, Bob seemed to be paying a lot more attention to the water ahead than the circumstances demanded. I should have known better. "It's going to get a little rough," he predicted with quiet understatement as we rounded the corner of Whale Island. As we passed out of its lee, we met a northerly breeze blowing briskly against the tide. In less than a minute, the water turned from glass to whitecaps to a chaotic jungle of irregular standing waves that practically swallowed the sky overhead. As Ernie Holland and I braced ourselves against the roll, Yaeger, Bob's imminently seaworthy Chessie, offered us a brief contemptuous look and left the cabin to scan the skies for ducks. Minutes later, the angry seas receded behind us as quickly as they had arisen and we continued on our way reminded that of all the duck hunting venues on earth, none makes you earn your shooting quite like Kodiak.

Back in calm water at the head of the bay, Ernie, Yaeger, and I hopped over the side and picked out a convenient driftwood log to use as a blind. As we arranged our makeshift quarters, Bob drifted with the tide, dropping a line of decoys just offshore at a depth calculated to give us an hour's worth of shooting before the falling tide left them high and dry. "Don't forget what we need for dinner!" he cried above the throb of the engine, and then he set off to attend to business in Port Lyons while Ernie, the dog, and I settled into the silence left behind.

We had dropped in to visit Bob armed primarily with bows and arrows, intent on a Sitka blacktail deer article for a bowhunting magazine in my case and a freezer full of venison in Ernie's. But we knew we could only battle grizzly-infested alders so long without a break, and we'd brought our shotguns along to fill in the down time between climbs up the mountains to the deer. But despite its apparently secondary nature, this was no ordinary duck hunt. In a fit of culinary pride, gauntlets had been thrown, and that week

Bob's Whale Pass Lodge had become the scene of the Great Alaska Duck-off.

To be honest, I'd never regarded cooking ducks as a competitive sport. But my old friend Ernie—former professional skier, soccer player, and rough-house boxer—is the kind of guy who can turn doing the dishes in hunting camp into a tournament. He's also the kind of guy who usually wins. But an inspired boast to the effect that his duck cooking was better than anyone else's in the world proved more than I could stand. And so with Bob, his wife, Denise, and my wife, Lori, recruited as impartial judges, we arrived equipped with everything we needed to settle the matter: four boxes of steel No. 2s and a cooler full of all the raw materials we could scrounge from the shelves of the grocery store on the way out of town.

All contests must have rules, and we reviewed them for the record as we huddled behind the log and waited for the ducks to start flying down from the head of the bay on the falling tide. No store-bought sauces allowed. No secret ingredients; all materials in the lodge kitchen were freely available to both contestants. Any attempt at jury tampering would result in immediate forfeit. And then there was the issue of the ducks themselves, for Kodiak waters support a truly remarkable assortment of waterfowl. Justifiably famous for its variety of sea ducks, Kodiak can show a hunter more species of waterfowl in one afternoon than most

146

of us will see in a season, if not a lifetime, from regulation-issue scoters and goldeneyes to harlequins and oldsquaws, and even, when the weather is really kicking offshore, four species of North Pacific eider. But in addition to these marine exotics, Kodiak also winters a surprising number of puddle ducks, including the largest, plumpest mallards I've ever seen in my life. Since a prime teal or mallard might unduly influence the judges, we agreed that we would each designate one duck from the other's bag at the end of the day, and that each of us would prepare that duck of the other's choosing for the nightly entry in the Duck-off. This decision left us strongly motivated to be careful in our shot selection.

By the time we had all this worked out, we were ready to get back to the innocent pleasures of duck hunting. An old hand at this game, Yaeger spotted the first inbound birds before we did. The noise they made as they whistled down the bay immediately identified them as goldeneyes: not the common variety familiar to the inland waters of the Lower 48, but stout Barrow's goldeneyes, crescent facial markings and faintly purple pates flashing in the autumn sun. The magnum decoys tacking back and forth against the tidal current proved enough to attract them, and as they tore past we rose and shot, leaving two drakes and a hen kicking in the sea. Never one to stand on ceremony, Yaeger was already halfway to the first fallen bird by the time the shots echoed away from the hills, but I found it hard to fault his lack of discipline. With the tide beginning to tear along in earnest, he had to swim a good quarter mile to complete the final retrieve.

"Which birds are yours?" Ernie asked as we dodged a shower of seawater from Yaeger and settled back into position behind the log.

"Beats me," I replied. "Take your pick."

"No...you take your pick." The Duck-off was young and we were still behaving like gentlemen. For a while.

Moments later, a pair of harlequins appeared around the point. I wanted a nicely plumaged drake for the taxidermist, and Ernie courteously offered me the shot. Few sea ducks

decoy as easily as harlequins, and as they set their wings over the blocks I rose and dropped the drake, providing Yaeger with a routine retrieve. He delivered the package in perfect condition without so much as a ruffled feather in its coat, and I placed the bird carefully on the log behind us.

When I spotted an inbound single heading toward us across the bay, it only seemed proper to repay Ernie's earlier courtesy, and I urged him to take the bird. His first shot kicked up a shower of water six feet behind the duck, and his second didn't come much closer. Since Ernie is a good shot, this performance should have alerted me to the possibility of something untoward, but the thought of dropping a duck Ernie had missed—twice—clouded my judgment. As I leveled the shotgun, I finally took a critical look at the quarry and pulled my barrels toward the sky.

"You missed on purpose!" I cried indignantly. "You tried to trick me into shooting so I'd have to cook a merganser!"

"Moi?" Ernie replied with a look of strained innocence that would have done justice to a Lab puppy caught in the garbage.

"I am shocked!"

"You told me to take it in the first place!" Ernie pointed out.

"It was half a mile away!" I protested. "I couldn't tell what it was."

Fortunately, a flock of surf scoters appeared before the charges of fraud could get out of hand. Ernie had just enough time to reload before they reached shotgun range. We rose and brought our guns up in unison. The falling tide had already left us noticeably farther from the waterline, but we still dropped three white-headed drakes belly up just beyond the decoys, and then it was time to watch Yaeger go to work again.

In contrast to most Labs, a breed that seldom performs well in the absence of their principal handler, Yaeger seemed perfectly content to hit the water even without Bob around. A typical Chessie, he left the impression that he was hunting for himself rather than for us, and I'm not sure he paid attention to anything I told him all afternoon. But despite his diffidence and enthusiasm for splattering us with seawater, we wouldn't have been able to do what we were doing without him, and I readily admit that I loved watching him tackle the cold sea beyond the beach with typical Chessie aplomb. And it's hard to argue with results. By the time Bob returned to pick us up for the ride back to Whale Pass, we had an impressive array of sea ducks resting on the log behind us, and thanks to Yaeger we hadn't lost a bird.

The feeling of hospitality any remote shelter provides depends as much on what's outside as on what lies between the walls. On the run back to the lodge, a layer of moist clouds blew in from Shelikoff Straight, eventually producing sheets of horizontal rain that lashed the boat as we plowed forward through the gloom. But Lori and Denise had the home fires blazing, and after we tended to the boat, the dog, the ducks, and the guns, we retreated to the *banya* to bake away the last of the rain and salt spray. By the time we finally gathered in the kitchen to begin the first round of the Duck-off, the rain lashing against the windowpanes only served to reinforce the comfort and security shared inside.

Some might hold that a wet retriever has no place inside a small living room with polite company, in which case I can only admit that none of us felt all that polite. Yaeger had certainly earned his laurels, and none of us begrudged him his place in front of the wood stove, even as the oily smell of damp Chessie began to permeate the lodge. After uncorking a bottle of cabernet to help chase away the last of the chill, I designated a goldeneye from Ernie's pile of ducks, and he pointed at a harlequin from mine. Then we rolled up our sleeves and went to work.

Perhaps it was the boisterous good company and perhaps it was the wine, but some doubt still remains as to the winner of the first round of the Duck-off. In his feistier moments, which aren't all that far apart, Ernie still contends that his Potted Goldeneye took top honors, and Bob, Denise, and Lori tend to diplomatic silence whenever the subject arises. But I know that deep down inside, Ernie's culinary tastes are too sophisticated to deny the obvious. He even admitted as much to me as we started up the mountain toward the deer the following morning...I think.

But whatever the contest's official outcome, we proved certain matters beyond a doubt: Sea ducks make good table fare, as long as they're prepared with enough imagination and served with enough wine; determined dogs in high seas provide one of the most stirring spectacles in outdoor sport; good company and a blazing stove can make a remote lodge feel like home even on the nastiest of nights.

Unlike contest results, some truths prove just too obvious to argue.

Chapter Fourteen

SOMETHING OUT OF NOTHING

Warm Indian summer air covered the marsh like a buffalo robe as the sun eased toward the western horizon. Insects buzzed lazily around the blind, while the decoys rested quietly upon the polished surface of the pond. Somewhere in the distance a lone red-wing called, and its rich churr seemed to carry forever through the stillness of the evening. Waterfowlers accustomed to stinging winds and wave-tossed decoy spreads might be forgiven for feeling out of place, but it was October in Montana, duck season was in progress, and I couldn't imagine a place I'd rather be.

The delicious tranquility the marsh offered felt even more inviting than the remote promise of birds in the air. Bathed in warm golden light, the prairie rolled up and away from the cattails in welcome layers of emptiness as far as the eye could see. Except for a dissolving contrail way off to the south and a few rectangles of wheat stubble etched against

155

the horizon, the landscape looked much as it must have looked to Lewis and Clark nearly two centuries earlier. After a long day of people and problems, I needed the respite the blind provided every bit as much as I needed the ducks that might or might not arrive after all.

The absence of one's fellow man may equate with solitude, but it does not necessarily mean being alone. As I relaxed and settled into the process of scanning the sky, the rich aroma of wet dog filled my nostrils, gradually replacing the marsh's fertile stink. Standing at the threshold of his first full season, Skykomish Sunka Zee wriggled eagerly beside me on the blind's rickety wooden seat, a helpless victim of the universal adolescent longing for action now as opposed to later. As soon as I clucked at him he settled down, subsiding into a warm, wet presence against my shoulder. The remarkable thing, I remember thinking at the time, was how little space a damp ninety-pound Lab really occupies, even one whose manners have yet to be tempered by experience.

I've endured my share of evenings fretting over the absence of ducks, but this wasn't one of them. I'd spent a typical day at the hospital, delivering unwelcome news to people who deserved better and trying to derive some redemption from small triumphs apparent to no one other than myself and a handful of friends. I really didn't need to shoot any birds that night. What I needed was silence and the freedom it implied. But the instant I saw the teal skimming in low across the cattails I knew that we had them, and I went into predator mode despite my contemplative mood.

Bluewings can embarrass experienced shooters even under the best of circumstances. As soon as I rose from the bench, the mud underfoot locked itself around my boots and gripped them like cement, which is my explanation for failing to convert the relatively easy double. By the time I dropped the first bird in the middle of the decoys, the flock had veered overhead, and when I tried to catch up with the second barrel I just couldn't twist around far enough to get the job done. As wingshooting excuses go, this one may not win any Pulitzer prizes, but that's my story and I'm sticking to it.

Despite all the long hours of training we had shared over the summer, I fully expected Sky to break at the sound of the first shot, but he surprised me. After offering a few choice expletives in the direction of the teal I'd missed and breaking open the gun, I found the dog still sitting on the bench behind me. But as soon as I whispered fetch, he launched over the top of the blind and churned his way out to the fallen teal, which he scooped up like an infielder snagging a ground ball. Breathing heavily in response to a sense of urgency apparent to no one but himself, he ducked under the wire front of the blind and delivered the bird to my hand without ruffling a feather.

Technically, of course, there was nothing to the retrieve. A kid could have done it, and in fact a kid just had. And if I had been hunting without a dog, I still would have claimed that first bird, at no greater cost than a few minutes of effort and the possibility of wet waders on a warm night when damp feet hardly mattered. But as I helped Sky clamor back up onto the bench and watched him settle into position, my intuition told me I had just witnessed a seminal event and that my life would never quite be the same again.

My intuition proved correct.

Let the truth be told: Under most circumstances, I wouldn't walk across the yard to shoot a duck unless I had a dog to retrieve it. Exceptions arise, of course, and we've looked at a few of them in earlier chapters, but they almost always involve the strong desire for a duck dinner in situations that preclude the presence of a dog. That's not waterfowling; it's shopping for food. There is a difference.

The retrieving breeds—especially Labs and Chessies—form such an integral part of the American waterfowling tradition that it's hard to imagine duck hunting's essential pageantry without them. There are practical considerations, of course; no responsible hunter feels comfortable killing game that cannot be recovered, and dropping ducks in icy water without the services of a capable retriever often amounts to little more than feeding the local scavengers. All involved parties deserve better, especially the ducks.

But a good dog's company means far more than increased efficiency as a hunter-gatherer. For most novice hunters, the excitement of the hunt derives primarily from the shooting. But as the technical aspects of knocking birds out of the sky become more routine, the inquisitive mind naturally seeks other sources of fascination. There comes a time when an eager Lab's heart-stopping water entry or the tenacity of an experienced Chessie pursuing a diver with a broken wing serves not as a footnote to the hunt but as the text itself. Despite our best efforts as trainers, dog work never becomes entirely predictable, and dogs always seem to find new ways to amaze and inspire us with their performance. The challenge of wingshooting may get new hunters into the duck blind in the first place, but it's the dogs that keep the fanatics coming back.

And they don't necessarily have to be dogs of championship quality. While I'm not involved personally with the field-trial circuit, I respect retriever trials for the standards they establish and the contributions those standards provide to the ongoing vigor of the retrieving breeds. Nonetheless, over the years some of the most memorable moments I've enjoyed in the duck blind have come courtesy of relatively unpolished retrievers that somehow found new ways to rise to the occasion. Tolerant attitudes like mine should not be construed as an excuse for intolerable behavior. No one enjoys hunting with an incorrigible hard-mouther or a dog

that cannot sit still when required. The point is simply that wonderful experiences with hunting dogs don't necessarily come courtesy of established champions.

Over the years, I've raised and trained several competent, hard-working Labs, but only one great one. And despite my own ability—shared by all but the most demanding retriever enthusiasts—to find admirable qualities in all those journeymen, I have to admit that the decade I hunted with the best felt qualitatively different from the rest of my waterfowling career. I hunted for Sky more than for myself, and I regarded every hunt primarily as an opportunity to watch him amaze me. Now all that seems impossibly long ago, before I was married to Lori or had children of my own.

But Lab people define their life passages by their dogs, and even though I wouldn't trade places with anyone as I enter my fifth decade of duck hunting, I'd trade anything— almost—to be able to hunt with Sky one more time.

With the single bluewing resting between us on the bench, the dog and I turned our attention back toward the evening sky. My contemplative mood had not survived the appearance of the teal. The bird I killed over the decoys reminded me how much I loved to shoot ducks, while my futile second shot left me twitchy and eager to redeem myself the next time around. After all, no batter likes to end the game on a strikeout. Besides, the single dead bluewing obligated me to pluck and clean without providing enough substance for a meal. The thought of even one more bird promised closure, and as the shadows began to creep across the marsh from the west, I did my best to conjure game from the still air overhead.

In contrast to the moth-winged teal, the next opportunity announced its arrival to the ear rather than the eye. Somewhere overhead a great tearing sound rent the air, but as I peered upward from the sheltering brim of my hat the sky remained stubbornly empty. As the noise rose to an improbable crescendo, I braced myself for the arrival of ducks in waves, a reasonable expectation that explains my surprise when the source of the disturbance finally declared

161

itself. Flaps extended like a Super Cub dropping into a tight mountain strip, a single mallard appeared out of the darkest quadrant of the sky, plummeting toward the decoys at a dizzying rate of descent. Even now it's hard to imagine all that noise arising from a lone set of wings.

Honest shooting light was failing fast, but I could still easily identify the sharp demarcation between dark thorax and light underbelly that marked the bird as a drake, and as he slid by high overhead I rose to take him. The bird shuddered as the sound of the shot spilled across the lonely marsh, but I realized at once that I hadn't killed him outright. Pivoting awkwardly, I tried to pick him up with the second barrel, but his momentum had already carried him out of range, leaving me with nothing to do but mark his course as he fluttered down toward the cattails.

Intensely irritated by my shooting, I broke open the gun and removed the live shell from the second barrel. Instead of ending the evening with a touch of class, I now faced the disturbing prospect of a lost bird. The retrieve would have been a challenge for an experienced dog under ideal conditions, and with daylight fading I considered cutting my losses and heading for home on the spot. But Sky looked eager, and motivated more by a sense of obligation than any expectation of success, I gave him the line and sent him over the top of the blind.

As the dog surged away in the direction of the fall, I left the empty shotgun behind on the bench and waded out toward the decoys. Sunset had brought a flurry of activity to the sky over the distant edges of the marsh, but I didn't have any more shooting left in me. Besides, I reasoned, if the dog was willing to give the retrieve his undivided attention, I owed him a certain measure of courtesy in return. And so I ignored the birds in the air overhead and stood unarmed in the decoy spread, idly gathering up blocks and following the progress of the retrieve with my ears. Given the thickness of the cover where the wounded drake had fallen, I knew there was nothing I could do to advance the cause. The bird had become the dog's to find or to lose.

Sky sounded like a water buffalo as he worked his way through the brittle reeds. At first he seemed to cast about methodically, but then I heard him hesitate, and the sound of cattails breaking yielded to the wet gurgle of a diving dog. Point and counterpoint, these two noises receded deeper and deeper into the depths of the cover, leaving me with the mental image of a wily bird trying to capitalize on a young dog's lack of experience. But Sky refused to abandon the chase, and as I worked my way through the process of gathering the decoys, the sound of pursuit faded slowly from the range of my hearing.

By the time I returned to the blind for the gun and the teal and started around the edge of the water with the decoy bag over my shoulder, the long day had faded to nothing but a dull brassy glow above the western horizon. Suddenly, the cattails parted and a widening wake appeared on the polished surface of the water, with its apex pointed in my direction. Relieved by the dog's reappearance, I didn't even realize what he had done until he bounded from the water and presented the mallard, which I accepted in a state of near disbelief. The warm, sleek feel of its plumage and the heft of the bird in my hand felt like some kind of miracle.

And just the first of many, as subsequent seasons proved. But spectacular canine performances have a unique way of liberating the observer from the urge to look forward in time to events that may or may not take place. Beyond any measure of ducks lost or recovered, good dogs ground us firmly in the present, the best of all possible times for hunters and dogs alike. And it is just that sense of immediacy that I remember as I walked out of the marsh with a duck dinner in the game vest and the dog trailing along at my side. Together we had made something out of nothing.

The rest could wait.

Chapter Fifteen

SEASON'S END

H ere on the high plains, sunrises assume a magical quality when the temperature dips below minus twenty. This morning, stars gleam like diamonds overhead. Silhouetted against the rising light, the edge of the horizon looks as if it has been traced by a laser. The air lies clear and still against the valley floor, leaving sounds amplified by the dense air's perfect acoustics: the babble of the creek, the crunch of hooves on ice as a whitetail doe makes her way across a frozen backwater, the eerie chorus of a coyote pack. The sky feels enormous, and not even the distant lights of town can dispel a certain sense of isolation. Only a fool would be out here on a morning like this, I remind myself as the air begins to sting the unprotected portion of my face between cap and scarf: a fool or a duck hunter. Years have passed since I last worried about trying to tell the difference.

But there is no remedy for lonely places quite like the company of an eager Lab, and as soon as I lower the tailgate, Sonny bounds forth to break the spell. He is an old dog now, but with all those seasons under his belt he knows full well what's up and he hits the ground like a puppy, frolicking and rolling through the snow in splendidly unnecessary play. Save it for later I long to advise him, but my impulse to restraint is as pointless as the little canine snow angels he's leaving behind in his wake. Never mind the ducks in the vest when the shooting is done...enthusiasm lies at the heart of the relationship between hunters and dogs, and I've learned enough myself by now not to compromise it.

By the time we've forged our way down to the creek the dog is all business, an attitude I wish I could somehow direct to the task of setting out the decoys. It's a trout stream, I remind myself in a deliberate attempt to evoke the memory of wading the same pool in cutoff jeans on balmy summer days. But it's all to no avail. Not even neoprene waders can soften the thought of setting out into the water on such a bitter morning. However, this is what we've come for, and after leaning the double up against a log and commanding the dog to sit, I stare at the water like an Olympic diver contemplating the view from the high board, and step off the bank.

At this point, the success of the hunt depends on my ability to set out the decoys without getting my hands wet. The digits are always the body parts most vulnerable to cold, and in this kind of weather, damp gloves will turn to wooly blocks of ice in seconds. Fortunately, on water this small a half dozen decoys will suffice. Working gingerly, I'm down to the last of six when I hear a wet slosh of water behind me. Sonny has decided to break command and help. Regrettably, "help" consists of swimming through the decoys, snaring two of the lines in the process. By the time I have the mess sorted out, our relationship has grown noticeably strained, but there is nothing to do but head for shore, cram my hands into my armpits, and hope the morning flight arrives before frostbite sets in.

Even by the standards of hardcore waterfowlers, the morning's undertakings may sound extreme, so a word of explanation seems in order. The creek is indeed a trout stream. In fact, it's one of Montana's true spring creeks, pouring out of a deep mountain aquifer at constant flow and temperature independent of season and weather. It never freezes, and the reassuring presence of open water it provides accounts for the population of mallards that winters here at this otherwise inclement latitude. And while this morning's exceptionally cold temperature may be an inconvenience, it is also a virtual guarantee of fast shooting to come, for frigid weather means solid ice on all the casual water elsewhere in the valley. On mornings like this the ducks will come, at least to those determined or stubborn enough to wait out their arrival.

However, my motivation today goes beyond the promise of classy shooting for fat, grain-stuffed mallards. Sonny is slowing down, and over the course of the long season I've had to confront the reality of his impending retirement. I would like to see him finish his career in style. Like any aging athlete, he deserves to go out a winner. And even if he isn't quite ready to call it quits, the season itself certainly is. It seems like only yesterday that we were swatting bugs under an Indian summer sun, waiting for the first flight of autumn to barrel in across the great fertile stink of a local marsh and wondering how we would survive the heat in our waders. But it wasn't yesterday; it was closer to three months ago. I still don't want it to end, in the same desperate way of not wanting something to end known only to hunters during the last week of the season and kids on the final day of summer vacation. Of course, hunting seasons and summer vacations always end, but that doesn't mean you have to take it lying down. Do not go gently, another Thomas once advised. Don't worry; I never planned to.

Despite it's psychological implications, it isn't getting into the water that kills you on mornings like this; it's getting out. The water temperature, after all, isn't really much different than it was when I last passed this way with fly-rod in hand. But the air above the creek is more than a hundred degrees colder, and within moments of my return to the bank my waders are coated with rime and Sonny is shivering at my side, his face framed by a corona of frosty whiskers. But he isn't whining. In fact, he's scanning the lightening sky for ducks: my kind of dog. And if he can stand it after all those years multiplied by seven, I ought to be able to as well.

Circulation restored, I ease my fingers through the tips of my cutoff gloves and load the gun gingerly, trying to avoid all contact between flesh and metal. I still remember the long-ago morning on a frigid day just like this when I decided to lick my gun barrel just to see what would happen, a maneuver that left me feeling as if I'd lost half my tongue. I suppose that's the kind of thing all kids try. Once.

Time never passes so slowly as it does when you're really cold, and I concentrate on studying our surroundings in order to distract myself. Just then the whole world literally turns to cooperate, shrugging its eastern shoulder just enough to let the sun ease into the sky at last. Fresh snow begins to sparkle. Encased in crystalline ice, the brush along the creek banks gleams like crown jewels. But before I can take it all in, the sound of tearing silk fills the still air to remind me of the difference between hunters and nature watchers. "Sit!" I remind the dog between clenched teeth, and then there is nothing to do but await developments.

Like Sonny, I've learned a few things over the years. When I hear the sound of setting wings but have no idea where the birds are coming from, I know enough to resist the temptation to look up, a natural impulse that usually results in nothing but flaring ducks. Instead, I keep my head down and wait, peering out from under the bill of my cap at the

171

decoys turning slowly in the current. This morning, discipline provides its own reward. Utterly at odds with the volume of the noise overhead, a single drake mallard appears downstream, gliding into the blocks with flaps fully extended. Gleaming in the cold morning light, the bird's iridescent green head practically demands the eye's attention, a single pixel of color framed against an otherwise stark background of black and white. I time my rise to take him twenty yards out, and the dead bird hits the water with a satisfying plop, while the sound of the shot echoes away toward the distant frozen hills.

Sonny launches at once, a violation of protocol I've allowed over the years as a concession to the demands of retrieving birds in moving water. The creek flows hard enough to sweep downed ducks away in a hurry, and I prefer to have retrieves in fast current play out in plain sight. Current can confuse even the best of dogs, but Sonny is an old hand at the game and he calculates the angle of interception perfectly, like a defensive back running down a wide-receiver in the secondary. Back on the bank, I accept the delivery and turn away from the inevitable shaking that follows. Circumstances don't allow much opportunity for reflection, for it's so cold that the bird has already started to stiffen.

But there is no time to worry about the crusty layer of ice forming on the drake's plumage. Informed by something unseen, flocks of birds have risen in mass from the grainfields above the creek, and the sound of chuckling mallards fills the air from all directions. Hunkering down with the wet dog against my side, I watch a tight formation of a dozen birds break over the top of the brush. Mentally isolating two drakes from the flurry of wings, I rise and drop them. Working nimbly, I reload as Sonny chugs downstream in pursuit. Not even the commotion of a dog in the water can keep the birds away this morning, and another pair lies kicking in the snow across the creek before he's finished the first retrieve.

It's a shame that it has to end so quickly, but the cold leaves little opportunity for regret. As much as I would love to stand and admire Sonny's workmanship, I leave the empty gun behind me on the bank and wade in to begin collecting the decoys while he's still in action. No offense intended; it's just too damn cold to endure any longer. Just as there is a time to stop and smell the roses, so there is a time to pack up and go, and that time has come. Somehow, I suspect the old dog will understand.

As we pack up and begin the walk back toward the sanctuary of the truck, the magical quality of the early light begins to yield to a snow-blind glare. Off in the distance, the sound of vehicles in motion rises from the roads as the town awakens to the rhythms of daily commerce. I never heard any shooting this morning other than my own, and it occurs to me that the dog and I have just shared a wonderful secret, the kind known only to those determined to test the limits of tolerance in the pursuit of all that is amazing about the outdoors.

Back at the truck, I heave the decoy bag over the tailgate and shed my game vest. Cased in icy feathers, the five-bird limit feels unnaturally heavy, and my back straightens pleasantly at the relief from the load. Sonny gathers his old legs to spring toward the kennel, but I invite him into the cab instead. He's earned a place next to the heater, and the aroma of a wet dog warming seems a cheap price to pay for the companionship we've shared today.

As we rattle back up the road toward home, I enjoy a sense of satisfaction beyond the measure of the birds resting in the back of the truck. The valley remains full of ducks. Sonny has held his retirement at bay. The season may be over, but the important things endure, ready for yet another season to follow as surely as tomorrow's sunrise.

CULINARY NOTES

I've taken the somewhat unusual step of punctuating this collection of hunting stories with cooking suggestions for two simple reasons: It's important for hunters to enjoy eating what they shoot, and many of people seem to have trouble with waterfowl in the kitchen.

I make no claim to real expertise as a chef, but given some dead ducks, a source of heat, and whatever adornments happen to be available in hunting camp, I can probably hold my own. And if there is a unifying theme to the cooking suggestions I've made, it's that waterfowl cooking problems don't arise because of deficiencies in complex cooking techniques. We usually fail with the simple elements of preparation, mainly as a consequence of overcooking.

Most waterfowl benefit from hanging. If weather conditions allow (or if you have access to a large cooler that allows plenty of air circulation), I recommend hanging all ducks and geese, undrawn, for four to six days.

Because of their high fat content, ducks and geese don't freeze as well as many game birds. I try to eat the waterfowl I shoot as soon as possible. If you've done well, invite friends over for dinner rather than filling the freezer with ducks that will not benefit from storage.

Birds meant for the oven should always be plucked rather than skinned. This extra bit of effort is unnecessary if you plan to use the filleted meat in a sautéed or highly seasoned preparation. When cleaning waterfowl for roasting, I like to split them along the backbone with a pair of heavy game shears. This allows easy cleaning of the body cavity and even heat distribution in the oven.

Prime waterfowl usually turn out best when roasted simply. However, you can't make beef Wellington out of chuck steak. If your bag consists of sea ducks or early-season birds studded with pin feathers, cut your losses, skin the birds, and use the meat in a bit more imaginative fashion (curry, stir-fry, teriyaki, Stroganoff...the possibilities are endless.) With a bit of enthusiasm in the kitchen, the results should still be delicious.

And remember that the nonhunting public's perception of hunters depends highly on the degree to which we use the game we kill. Learning to cook waterfowl competently isn't just good for the dinner table. It's good for the sport.

Chapter 2: Grilled Duck

Cooking ducks over an open grill can be tricky because of the danger of overcooking. However, the results can be spectacular, especially if you are fortunate enough to enjoy a good supply of an even-burning wood such as mesquite. Because of variations in cooking temperature and meat thickness, prescribing precise cooking times is impossible, and the cook will have to rely on his or her judgment at the time. Because of their higher ratio of surface area to mass, smaller ducks are easier to cook uniformly over coals than are large birds such as mallards. When cooking a number of birds for company, I usually pull one off to the side and sample it at frequent intervals. The goal should be a bird with the consistency of a medium-rare steak—sizzling on the outside, with a warm, pink center.

Mesquite Grilled Wigeon

1/2 cup olive oil	juice from 3 fresh lemons
1/2 tsp. cumin	4 pintails
2 tsp. fresh cilantro	3 cloves garlic, crushed
	salt and crushed red pepper to taste

1. Split birds lengthwise along the backbone with game shears. Press flat with heel of hand.
2. Combine remaining ingredients and marinate ducks in ceramic bowl for four hours.
3. Arrange birds in wire basket and grill over mesquite coals until cooked according to earlier guidelines.

CHAPTER 5: WILD GOOSE

Now what to do with all those geese? The question
assumes new significance now that hunters can come home
with twenty legal snows a day. An honorable disposition
seems especially important given the public scrutiny the new
extended seasons and liberal bag limits are sure to receive.
After all, eating geese provides the justification for addressing
the overpopulation problem with shotguns instead of more
politically correct means.

Geese on the table arouse more varied opinions than any
other subject in wild game cookery. I know several avid waterfowlers who avoid shooting them simply because they don't like
to eat them. Too bad; while geese can be unpleasantly tough,
they can also provide excellent eating. As is usually the case with
waterfowl, unpalatable geese are more often the product of overcooking than any problem with the raw material.

My parents taught me at an early age that ducks and geese
should always be plucked whole, a wise maxim that circumstances forced me to ignore on my trip to Colorado. After all,
you can only fit so much wild goose in a suitcase, and the air-
lines weren't likely to let me carry the rest along on a game
strap. But I had promised Lori a goose dinner the night I
returned home, and despite the demands of my travel schedule
I delivered. Breasted geese allowed the simple preparation
described below, which earned enough points on the home
front to forestall any complaints about my absence.

Snow Goose Breasts in Currant Sauce

breasts from 2 snow geese	1/4 cup soy sauce
2 tbsp. butter	2 tbsp. red currant preserves
1 tbsp. balsamic vinegar	1/4 cup red wine
1 tbsp. freshly grated ginger	

1. Fillet goose breasts from carcass, saving legs for stock.
2. Marinate goose breasts in soy sauce for 4 to 6 hours.
3. Melt butter in sauce pan. Add preserves, wine, vinegar, and ginger. Mix and warm over low heat.
4. Sear goose breasts on grill over high heat until crisp on the outside and medium rare in the center, approximately 6 minutes per side.
5. Remove cooked goose breasts to warmed platter, cover with sauce, and serve with wild rice.

Chapter 6: Roast Mallard

While roast mallard remains a mainstay of wild game cookery, this basic dish causes more than its share of frustration. Remember that sauce is just icing on the cake, and no amount of artistry in that department can overcome an improperly cooked bird. The usual culprit is overcooking, an error that results in something that tastes like tough liver instead of wild duck. Most hunters who complain about wild duck on the table have simply never eaten duck that wasn't overcooked.

In general, ducks should be roasted uncovered in a hot oven (475 degrees) for short periods of time. Of course timing is critical, because at high oven temperatures a few minutes can mean the difference between perfection and disaster. Unfortunately, it's hard to offer generic cooking times because all ovens differ in their capacity to deliver heat at any given thermostat setting. There are two simple solutions to this problem. The first is to use a reliable meat thermometer. Generally, duck tastes best cooked to an internal temperature around 130 degrees, although individual preferences will vary between 120-140. I also recommend "calibrating" your own oven just like a shooter sighting in a rifle. Place four mallards of equal size on a roasting pan in a fully preheated oven and remove them quickly at two-minute intervals beginning at 18 minutes. The birds should come out varying between the equivalent of rare and medium beef. Note which best suits your taste and target that cooking time in the future. When cooking smaller birds, remember to adjust cooking time downward (or use a meat thermometer).

CHRIS TAYLOR'S ROAST MALLARD

3 fresh oranges	1 fresh grapefruit
1/4 cup Marsala	1/2 cup honey
1/4 cup red wine	1/2 tsp. ground cloves
1/8 cup plus 2 tbsp. Grand Marnier	1/2 tsp. allspice
1/8 cup plus 2 tbsp. cognac	2 green chilies
1 can mandarin oranges	3 tbsp. Dijon mustard
dash Worcestershire, salt, pepper	4 plucked mallards

1. Press juice from fresh oranges and grapefruit. Grate orange rind and save.
2. Combine chilies and mandarin oranges in blender.
3. Season ducks with 1/4 cup honey, Worcestershire, and mustard rubbed into skin.
4. Prepare topping from orange rind, 2 tbsp. each honey, cognac, and Grand Marnier.
5. Combine fruit juices, wines, spices, chili-orange mixture and remaining brandies and honey. Simmer over low heat.
6. Baste ducks liberally with above mixture and roast according to previous discussion.
7. Remove cooked birds, carve breasts and legs from carcasses, and serve over steamed spinach with topping and remaining sauce.

CHAPTER 7: TEAL

With conviction certain to arouse argument in some circles, I'll go on record as saying I would rather eat prime bluewing teal than any other game bird in North America. Sweet, fine-grained, and succulent, teal require little elaboration in the kitchen. Their small size makes them easy to overcook, and cooking times should generally be reduced by approximately 30 percent in comparison to larger puddle ducks. A honey glaze will help retain moisture.

HONEY ROASTED TEAL

6 plucked teal	2 tbsp. fresh grated ginger
2 tbsp. soy sauce	2 tbsp. sesame oil
1/2 cup honey	

1. Combine soy, oil, and ginger. Rub into duck breasts and let stand 1 hour.
2. Warm honey in microwave until liquid. Brush onto duck breasts.
3. Roast birds on open rack in hot oven until crisp on the outside, approximately 15 minutes.

CHAPTER 8: HILLARY SHELDON'S MINCED DUCK
(This is my own slightly modified version of her recipe)

4 duck breasts   **1/2 cup mutton fat**
1/2 tsp. sage   **1/2 tsp tarragon**
2 tbsp. bread crumbs   **dash salt, black pepper**

1. Fillet duck breasts and soak 1 hour in salted water.
2. Run breasts and fat through meat grinder. Mix thoroughly with bread crumbs and spices.
3. Shape ground meat into patties and grill over high heat until medium rare in the center.
4. Serve hot with roasted new potatoes and tossed green salad.

CHAPTER 10: SNIPE

I like to hang snipe for several days, weather permitting. They are quite easy to pluck, and plucking (as opposed to skinning) adds considerably to their table quality. Because of their small size, snipe lend themselves better than most waterfowl to skillet cookery, a convenience when cooking in the field without an oven.

PAN FRIED SNIPE

6 plucked snipe	3/4 cup seasoned flour
6 strips bacon	1 white onion

1. Cut snipe along backbone and flatten with heel of hand.
2. Dredge birds in seasoned flour and set aside.
3. Chop bacon and heat in well-seasoned cast-iron skillet until crumbly; remove with slotted spoon.
4. Dice onion and cook in bacon grease until translucent. Remove and add to bacon.
5. Pan-fry snipe over medium-high heat until medium rare at center of breast, approximately 4 minutes per side.
6. Combine with bacon and onion and correct seasoning with dash salt and freshly ground pepper.

CHAPTER 11: ROAST GOOSE

As discussed earlier, geese cause more problems than any other subject in game cookery. That's a shame, for prime goose properly prepared can be a delight. Above and beyond the usual problem of overcooking, older birds tend to be tough. Young geese usually have notched tail feathers. That obviously isn't much help on the wing, but in the hand young birds should be saved for roasting while older specimens are better cooked in other ways (by filleting the breasts and cooking the meat in a crock pot, for example).

Because of their larger body size, geese should be roasted in a cooler oven than ducks to allow even heating (375 degrees). A meat thermometer can be very helpful when roasting geese because of the variability in their size. Aim for an internal temperature of 130 degrees. When stuffing geese, draw them by cutting along the backbone. This allows easy but thorough cleaning of the body cavity. After stuffing the birds, close the slit along the back with skewers prior to cooking.

ROAST GOOSE WITH APRICOT-SAUSAGE STUFFING

2 plucked young Canada geese
dash salt, pepper
1 finely chopped onion
1 1/2 cups breadcrumbs
1/2 tsp. fresh thyme

1 lemon
2 tbsp. butter
2 lbs. lean game sausage
2 cans apricots, chopped
1/4 tsp. ground nutmeg
8 tbsp. heavy cream

1. Rub goose breasts with lemon quarters; sprinkle with salt and pepper.
2. Melt butter in large saucepan. Saute onion over medium heat until clear.
3. Add sausage; crumble and brown.
4. Add apricots, breadcrumbs, and seasonings. Cook over low heat for five more minutes
5. Remove from heat and blend in cream. Correct seasoning.
6. Spoon stuffing mixture into body cavities of geese. Save remainder in small casserole dish and place in oven along with geese.
7. Pre-heat oven to 425 degrees. Cook on open roasting pan at 375 degrees to internal temperature of 130 degrees.

CHAPTER 13: SEA DUCKS

Ducks vary tremendously as table fare and the approach to their preparation should vary as well. While species such as teal, mallard, and pintail require a minimum of fuss in the kitchen, others demand a bit more cooking. Sea ducks probably enjoy the lowest culinary reputation of all waterfowl, and that's unfortunate. They aren't really bad; they're just different, and they need to be prepared accordingly.

The fat layer beneath the skin tends to concentrate the taste of whatever ducks have been eating, so I usually skin sea ducks just to eliminate that variable from the equation. Most sea ducks have relatively lean breasts, and I prefer to fillet them and cook the meat in strips. Marinating the meat even briefly helps improve both taste and texture. And while prime puddle ducks taste so good unadorned that it's almost a shame to mask their flavor, sea ducks usually benefit from some seasoning.

Hot Ginger Harlequin

2 filleted harlequin breasts	2 tbsp. soy sauce
2 tbsp. freshly grated ginger	1/2 tsp. sugar
1/2 tsp. rice vinegar	2 tbsp. sesame oil
dash hot chili oil	1 tsp. cornstarch

1. Skin and breast ducks. (Heresy, I know, but these are sea ducks.) Slice breast meat into thin strips.
2. Combine soy, ginger, sugar, vinegar, and chili oil. Marinate duck in mixture for one hour. Drain, saving marinade.
3. Heat sesame oil in wok and stir-fry duck over high heat, taking care not to overcook.
4. Combine remaining marinade with cornstarch. Add to duck and heat until glazed.
5. Serve with crackers as appetizer, or over steamed rice as a side dish.

PEOPLE AND PLACES

As the preceding text should make clear, I'm pretty much a do-it-yourself kind of guy in the outdoors. However, I have a number of friends in the guiding and outfitting business, and in order to facilitate those who might like to share in some of these experiences, I would like to make the following contact information available.

Chapter 5. John Eden offers both traditional autumn waterfowling and extended-season snow goose hunting on vast track of land on the plains of eastern Colorado. Contact him at 110 N. Main St., Lamar, CO 81052; 719-336-4303.

Chapter 6. My neighbors Chris and Rick Taylor offer food, lodging, and dog care through their Pheasant Tales Bed and Bistro. Contact them at RT 1, Box 1615, Lewistown, MT 59457; 406-538-2124.

Chapter 8. Doug and Hillary Sheldon provide delightful accommodations, wingshooting, and fishing at their Foveran Station on New Zealand's South Island. Book through Kiwi Safaris, P.O. Box 270079, Christchurch, NZ; email Mike.Freeman.Kiwi.Safaris.NZ@xtra.co.nz

Chapter 13. Legendary Kodiak bear guide Bob May would really rather hunt ducks than big game. He and his wife, Denise, operate Whale Pass Lodge on the north side of the island. Contact them at P.O. Box 32, Port Lyons, AK 99550; 800-4-KODIAK.